An Angel on my Shoulder

Alaereba Stella Ikiriko

Onwards and Upwards Publishers

3 Radfords Turf,
Cranbrook,
Exeter,
EX5 7DX,
United Kingdom.
www.onwardsandupwards.org

This first edition published in the United Kingdom by Onwards and Upwards Publishers (2017).

ISBN: 978-1-911086-86-4
Typeface: Sabon LT
Editor: Victoria Lyle
Graphic design: LM Graphic Design

Printed in the United Kingdom.

Endorsement

In this book, Alaereba Stella Ikiriko has shared the unique story of the process of her coming to faith in Jesus. What makes this book remarkable is that she opens to us the inner conversations of her mind and heart. We all have such conversations as we listen to our hopes, questions, fears, commitments and loves, as we try to make sense of our present situation. From her experience, Alaereba encourages us to find the quiet and persistent voice of God among the other inner voices and emotions.

For her, the voice of God made His presence real; especially in the challenges she faced – like the many nights when every breath was a physical ordeal as she lay sleepless, longing for morning.

I commend this book because of Alaereba's honesty and valuable insights. It has alerted me afresh to listen for the voice of God in the inner conversations of my soul and to be assured of his presence. May it be a similar blessing to you.

Rev. Dr James Dainty
Chester Diocese, 2016

About the Author

Alaereba Stella Ikiriko (known as Stella) has been a qualified nurse and midwife for forty-five years. She came to the UK in 1975 to train as a midwife at St Luke's Maternity Hospital in Bradford, West Yorkshire, and was one of the pioneer midwifery students that trained in a new one year Integrated Midwifery curriculum.

After eighteen months of gaining post qualification experience in the UK she returned home to Nigeria to practise in a Government Hospital setting as Staff Nurse Midwife. She then decided to return to the UK again to pursue her vision as a professional midwife which was a unique opportunity that was not available at the time for dual qualified midwives in her home country.

In June 1990 she came back to the UK to fulfil that vision and was employed in one of the UK reputable Obstetrics and Gynaecology hospitals in West London. She acquired new skills which motivated her to take up her career as a more skilled practitioner to an autonomous Caseload (One to One) midwifery practice. This entailed huge responsibilities; despite that, the experience was always rewarding. She excelled in Caseload Practice, working with often very vulnerable women in the community, and she retired in April 2011.

"In thirty-five years of professional practice, can I put a figure to the number of babies I delivered safely into the world? The answer is no!" says Stella.

"In retirement, what I enjoy in my Faith are the joy and peace that come with trusting Jesus each dawn, holding onto Him as my Lord and personal Saviour. Amen."

To contact the author, please write to: *alaiki@talktalk.net*

Contents

An Angel on my Shoulder

Foreword by Philip Quenby

When was the last time an angel appeared from nowhere and told you what to do in an emergency? Or a mysterious man in white approached you with instructions for healing a long-standing illness? Most of us are prepared to admit that there are things in life that are beyond scientific explanation, but we often baulk at some of the wilder claims about the supernatural. Quite rightly so, for though there are many instances of extraordinary things happening to ordinary people, there is sadly no shortage of outlandish tales spread by charlatans and hucksters. In trying to sort truth from falsehood, a degree of scepticism is in order; there is nothing wrong in applying the same tests for this that we use in other walks of life, but it would be foolish to disregard possibilities just because they lie outside the range of our own personal experience. This book contains the eyewitness testimony of a woman who has seen angels and experienced miraculous events. One question above all others is likely to strike any reader who has not had similar things happen to them: why should we take her word for it?

To that I offer a one-word answer: integrity. If someone has consistently shown that their judgment can be relied on and their word has always been true, then they deserve a careful hearing even if they are speaking about a world beyond the normal powers of apprehension of our senses. Though I was not party to the events described, integrity is something I can vouch for. I have been privileged to know Stella Ikiriko for over ten years, have seen her in good times and in bad, have shared with her in many different situations and have seen how she acts towards people from all walks of life. The story that unfolds in the pages of this book will give readers a chance to learn something of her character, the experiences that have moulded her and her reliability as a witness. For myself, I believe her to be utterly trustworthy, possessing the natural exuberance and warmth which characterises many of her fellow countrymen and women, but lacking any trace of suggestibility, superstition or hysteria – exactly as we might expect with someone pursuing such a no-nonsense career as midwifery.

If this eyewitness testimony is reliable and the events to which Stella testifies are true (as I believe them to be), then it is only right to ask a question of ourselves, too: what does all this mean – is it a diverting story or should it change the way we see the world and the God who made it? The deity Stella talks about has not turned His back on what He created, but daily shows His care for each human being, longing to meet with us so that we may build a relationship of love with Him. He is a miracle-working God, but does not ask us to leave our intellects behind when we come before Him. Quite the opposite: he wants us to use our brains He has given, saying, "Come, let us reason together." (Isaiah 1:18). As you reflect on Stella's story, I invite you to reason about how the things she describes can be, what these disclose about the Creator of the universe and what they mean for us, whom He crafted with infinite care and skill to glorify Him and to enjoy Him forever.

Philip Quenby
Author of 'Redeeming a Nation' and 'Moses and Pharaoh'

Introduction

This is a story of transformation. It is my story, but also the tale of an amazing, miracle-working God. It is a journey from the villages of Nigeria to the great metropolis of London, yet much more besides: a voyage from orphan childhood to recognising myself to be the daughter of a loving heavenly Father; from bereavement and brokenness towards increasing wholeness; from anxiety in the face of pressing earthly troubles to security in the embrace of the creator of the universe. This change did not come about overnight, and it was certainly not always easy. There have been many mistakes and wrong turns along the way, with times when it seemed I was travelling backwards instead of forwards. It is not something I could have brought about in my own strength or through human strategies. I look back with amazement at what God has achieved, full of thanks for His kindness and love in granting me spiritual and physical well-being when I was lost in darkest sorrow and despair.

I have come to know the Almighty God and what He did for me through Jesus in a slow but sustained process that eventually transformed my life – a faith revelation. I share some of these experiences in the pages that follow. Much of what I relate may appear ludicrous or fictitious, yet every word is true. Jesus did for me exactly what He said He would. My hope and prayer is that this journey will encourage, inspire and reassure others, especially those facing difficult times. Life is always a roller coaster, the twists and turns of unforeseen circumstances one moment bringing robust peace, the next intolerable pain. I have learnt that walking through these challenges with the One who made us for relationship with Him makes all the difference.

It comes as a great surprise to me to be writing a book. Since returning from pilgrimage to Israel in October 1997, I have kept prayer journals to document intercessions, encounters with Jesus, inspirations and prayers. Occasionally I have shared some of these with friends and family and I have learnt a lot from them in my personal life and faith journey. I see them as gifts from God and as part of His blessing on my life, so I have always prayed to be shown how to use them for His purposes. In January 2016 that prayer was answered as I was watching a programme on a Christian television network, when I clearly sensed God telling me, "This is the time" – the time to share my story more widely, to witness about the Good News and to tell how I have encountered Jesus along my own personal road to Emmaus. The conviction that this was what I was called to do was confirmed and strengthened as I attended Pentecost celebrations in London later the same year, and what you have before you is the result. May you be blessed as you read it.

CHAPTER ONE

Upbringing

I was born and bred on a small island called Buguma, in Rivers State in the Federal Republic of Nigeria – one of many islands in the Delta formed by tributaries of the River Niger. The strategic position of Buguma makes it of great importance in crude oil and gas production, though this is by no means an unalloyed blessing: any advantage that may accrue in terms of contribution to national wealth is offset by sporadic violence by insurgents and their periodic abduction of oil company staff, as well as by pollution in the creeks from illegal drilling and spillage of crude oil. Nigeria remains a fractured society where the primary loyalty is to tribe and family, a legacy that is exacerbated by poor government and corruption, and these issues are brought starkly into focus by arguments over how revenues from natural resources should be allocated. Oil wealth, which should be a benefit, has too often seemed a curse – to my people and to the country as a whole.

My people are the Ijaw tribe, a minority ethnic group in the Delta South of Nigeria. We are known as Kalabari and have our own separate Kalabari language. Before the discovery and exploration of crude oil, the main occupation of the Kalabari was fishing – not only in the creeks but also out in the Atlantic Ocean. As in many African countries, Nigerians live in extended families, and the Kalabari are no exception, with clusters of families grouped together under the same roof as one household. The family unit as a whole takes responsibility for the daily running of the household, with care of younger family members being managed by older generations, reflecting the ancient African proverb that says, "It takes a village to raise a child." There is wisdom in this

11

and many good things about this system, though it can involve unwelcome interference into each other's lives – marriages, dress codes, even procreation. Nevertheless, people accepted this as normality and nobody would have dared to complain or criticize these traditional ways, for rudeness and insolence from the young were simply not tolerated. Even though the drastic public punishments of the past have long been abolished, the social stigma associated with such disrespectful behaviour remains to this day.

I was a beneficiary of this system since my older brother and I were orphaned at a young age. I have no memory of my father, so what I know of him comes from what I was told by my mum, stepmum and older siblings. I was only a year old and my brother two years old when our dad died. I was the eleventh of his twelve children; my older brother and I were of the same mother. Our mum also died young, leaving her two much-loved children in the care of her own mother and two older brothers. That was how good the extended family system can be in times of need. It turned out to be a blessing for my brother and me. Our grandmother died a year after her own daughter's demise, yet we were loved and cared for, being given an admirable (albeit firm) upbringing by our maternal uncles and having the chance to gain good academic qualifications. So, despite being an orphan, when I was growing up I experienced the warmth and influence of family, and the discipline of my elders, even if not necessarily of my biological parents. We were taught always to live up to the standards expected of us, respecting the status and values of the family – rules that had to be honoured, come what may. Nobody ever questioned this because disobedience merited six strokes of the cane on the palm of the hand, on the legs or directly on the buttocks, depending on the age of the culprit. It was as though everyone carried a banner of responsibility to maintain the integrity, role and status of the family in our community and the villages roundabout, and must avoid anything that would bring shame on us.

Our family was not affluent by Nigerian standards, but we were respected and God-fearing with a rich cultural heritage, and were seen as people to look up to both in our own village and in others nearby. We were brought up to be content with whatever we had, to be grateful for God's providence and ready to share with others what little we had to spare. We were taught to know and fear God, to keep the Ten

Commandments[1] and to think of the Almighty as our Father in heaven. We memorized the Lord's Prayer and the Apostles' Creed by heart, both in our own dialect and in English. These were recited daily during devotions at home and at school, and during church services on Sundays. Misusing the Word of God was regarded as an abomination, the Bible being accepted unquestioningly as an inspired holy book. Even the presence of a bible was seen as manifesting the healing power of God, so that if someone were very ill, the habitual reaction was to place it under the sick person's pillow. This practice was so much the accepted norm that even medical professionals respected it and would think nothing of finding a bible under a patient's pillow in hospital. Some people refused to take an oath on the Bible to claim their innocence because they believed that God punishes and kills a liar – indeed, even those who worshipped other gods had an underlying fear of "the God in heaven". Spiritual things were thus very much part of everyday life.

Despite what some in the West might think, civilisation is well advanced through education, travel and intermarriage across most of the African continent. We may appear to be imperfect with regards to democracy on the world stage, but we nevertheless have traditions that reflect the impact of God on our beliefs. So, for example, it is common to have thanksgiving services to make an offering to God as a mark of gratitude, whether in times of joy or sorrow. Such services are regular tokens at the start of a new phase of life, such as when a new baby is born, promotion gained at work, success obtained in business, when there is convalescence after ill-health or as a memorial for those who have died. In the Asaritoru Local Government Area of Rivers State, where I come from, a new mother is not expected to have any public engagement until she has been to church to make a thanksgiving offering, particularly for her first birth. This is a paramount responsibility of her parents and husband, and both families embrace it equally. It proclaims allegiance to the all-knowing God who has control over life and death and is a prominent feature of our society, particularly among the Kalabari. It is, of course, true that a lot of superstition still exists alongside these traditions, and many people continue to visit soothsayers, traditional witch doctors and fortune tellers, but the overall atmosphere is honouring to God.

---

[1] See Exodus 20

Public celebration of the main Christian festivals was thus an unavoidable part of my upbringing, marking the passing of the seasons and major events, and reminding everyone of the central truths of the faith that remains an important part of Kalabari life to the present day. Christianity is still a big part of our community tradition and upbringing: most families have faith in the Almighty God, creator of all things, and pay no heed to superstitious beliefs or the power of witchcraft, though these are predominant practices within Nigerian culture and society as a whole. The events of Easter, in particular, are taken very seriously. Good Friday is a day of mourning for all Christians, just as one would mourn for the dead in a family. Everyone wears black clothes until Easter morning. In our household, if my elder uncle ("Papa", as we used to call him) heard any noise, the culprit was sure to be punished. In this way I came to experience Good Friday as the day Jesus, God's own Son, died. I still wear black clothes on Good Fridays and treat it as a reminder of who I was before Jesus died on my behalf.

Easter Eve is likewise very special in my local community at home. At the end of the wake at midnight, the church bells call everyone to assemble for Easter carols and there is singing and dancing around the village in preparation to meet the risen Jesus on Sunday morning. We knock on the doors and windows, waking up those who are sleeping, and inviting them to be part of the Easter carol procession. Nobody gets angry; some donate to good causes while others join the procession for the joy of proclaiming the Good News of the resurrection of Jesus from death. Easter Sunday celebration comes with general and individual thanksgiving by groups and families as a mark of appreciation for God's care and provision. After a lengthy time of thanksgiving, prayers and worship, families then go home to enjoy sumptuous meals. The great attraction for children was having a new outfit to wear on Easter Sunday. Easter and Christmas are celebrated alike among Christians in Nigeria.

Papa was a primary school headmaster and an Anglican church lay reader. He was very stringent about the family's religious values and strict about keeping the sabbath; nobody was allowed to do manual chores at home on the holy day, so Sunday meals were cooked on Saturday evenings. He was lovely, but uncompromising in his methods of discipline. As a result, that was exactly what I believed God, the heavenly Father, was like. It was scary! Although my upbringing gave me good foundations, what I thought Christianity involved at this time was quite different from what I understand now. The emphasis then was on the power and justice of God at the expense of His love and mercy. It was a message reinforced by the culture in which I grew up. In most religious beliefs and practices, people worship God as the superior deity and each sect believes that He is the supreme and the most powerful creator of all things. In Nigeria, for example, we have about two hundred spoken languages and each ethnic group has a totally different name for God, but all of them denote His supremacy with words such as mighty, creator, king, possessor, ruler and father, to name just a few. (The huge diversity in language is why pidgin English was adopted as a common tongue throughout the whole Republic of Nigeria. Since language was also a barrier in communication between the colonial masters and the indigenous people, English was made compulsory in education from primary school level upwards and a pass in English language was needed in order to qualify for an O-level certificate.)

One thing for which I am hugely grateful to Papa is that he put no obstacles in the way of my education. A few generations before mine, women's education was seen as irrelevant. African culture and tradition saw a woman's place as being at home so that she could serve her husband and his household and produce children. As a result, many women were uneducated. In my day, some of us started to challenge this approach, but it will take many generations to eradicate it completely. Even today it causes many marriages to fail, as some men still find it difficult to accept gender equality as a necessity in building up strong and respectful future generations. (Attitudes like this may also have contributed to the diminished position of women in politics and governance in Africa compared to the developed countries.)

At any rate, these prejudices did not prevent me from pursuing my selected course. I chose the nursing profession, which most girls aspired to. Nursing was a lucrative vocation everywhere in the world and was exceptionally competitive in Nigeria. Having a high grade in the entrance examination was a necessity for gaining admission into a higher institution of learning. I trained and qualified as a State Registered Nurse at the School of Nursing University College Hospital Ibadan in the former Western State of Nigeria, now called Oyo State. Our schedule and curriculum were the same as for the equivalent qualification licensed by the General Nursing Council for England and

Wales because the college was recognized by the council as having an excellent standard of nursing education. This provided the opportunity for prospective students to train and be qualified in the UK as State Certified Midwives (SCM), after qualifying as State Registered Nurses in Nigeria. Meanwhile, my brother was employed by Shell-BP after qualifying for his O-level certificate and, in time, we were able to contribute towards supporting our uncles and the younger generation of the family. To be fair to our uncles, we had no obligation to support them financially with our meagre income, but it was a gesture of appreciation, joy and gratitude for investing in a nephew and niece they had brought up with their own scanty resources. My brother saved to go to the USA to study petroleum engineering at the University of Oklahoma, but my future lay in a different direction.

CHAPTER TWO

Setting Out

I had never seen snow before and now snowflakes were tumbling from the sky. I had come to Britain in December 1974, enrolled at the Midwifery School at St Luke's Maternity Hospital in Bradford, West Yorkshire, and started my midwifery training in January 1975. Here I was on my first trip outside Nigeria, experiencing a proper English winter – something that always made me homesick because of the contrast with what I was used to at home. The scene outside the classroom window looked so strange and foreign. It reminded me of my secondary school plant biology lessons on the budding system of plants in winter.

"Do you like the snow?" It was one of my classmates, a Malaysian girl, speaking.

"Yes," I replied, expecting her to ask if I had seen snow before, but she seemed to assume I had and did not ask any more questions.

"Where is your umbrella?" asked another colleague.

"I did not realise that it was snowing when I left the hostel," I answered, not wanting to show my ignorance. In Nigeria we use umbrellas for protection from intense sunshine. I had no idea they could be used in the snow.

Naturally enough, people thought we would know this sort of thing. It was hardly the job of the hospital management to educate foreign students about the unpredictable British weather! I determined to be open-minded about this new culture and its people, and I quickly learnt that many things I had been told about Britain and her people were different from the reality. There were many contrasts with Nigeria. One of the most difficult things to get used to was the transition from the friendly, open and integrated society I had grown up in to a much more individualistic (and lonely) way of life. At first the freedom was exhilarating. I was able to make my own decisions without depending on someone else, having to take account of others' expectations or being bound by cultural norms. It felt like a breath of fresh air. I knew that I was responsible for myself, that I must focus on the purpose for which I had come to the UK and that I would have no one else to blame if I made mistakes. Life was more pleasant in a democratic system where there is freedom of speech for all – British and immigrants have same right to vote in national elections once your name is entered on the electoral register. Yet, despite this, I still missed home.

We had nice and supportive lecturers who gave that extra bit of their time when they realised that I was an A-grade student with first-rate training. I consolidated my post-qualification experience within eighteen months and returned to Nigeria. Everything in my life looked to be unfolding well. I was happy, successful and contented in my career and comfortably accepted in the community and culture in which I had been born and bred. I was, by now, a married woman and seemed to have the world at my feet. Yet things are seldom as straightforward as we would like them to be. Pain and upheaval were lying in wait.

Tears coursed down my cheeks as I knelt on the bedroom floor praying; tears of anger, pain and low self-esteem. It was a Friday morning and I did not know where to turn. All my hopes had turned to dust and the high promise of my early years had seemingly evaporated. My marriage was being torn apart – by bitterness, jealousy and hatred. Little did I know when I returned to Nigeria what emotional pressures would confront me in my marital home, putting unbearable strain on the relationship with my husband. My brother had seen what was coming and, though he did not want to interfere, he told me, "Come home to me if you think enough is enough." He loved me so much that he never wanted me to be upset for any reason and was unfailingly truthful and supportive. The love of my brother was what I always saw as my anchor and he was my role model. It was not easy for me to break away from an emotional relationship, but there was no other option. I left my marital home for good.

Now I cried out in anguish to my Maker, though I did not know exactly what to say to Him. The habits of thought I had learnt in my early years were difficult to erase and I was always fearful of coming before God.

Suddenly a voice called me by my African name: "Alaereba!"

I looked around. There was no one else in the room.

"Get up from the floor," the voice continued. "Wipe away your tears. I will fight your fight for you."

I knew it was the Lord calling me. The Almighty, the God who had always seemed so distant and scary, had taken note of my distress and had spoken to me by name – words of kindness and encouragement, the sort of words a loving father would speak.

From that moment I became confident, courageous and strengthened in God's mighty power, no longer fearful of striking out on my own as a single woman. My outlook was transformed and the overwhelming anger, disappointment and emotional trauma I had felt disappeared instantly. I did not rush over new plans but was relaxed and carried on with my job as normal, though now I had a focus on what would come next and an open mind about a potential change of environment. Whilst there were other possibilities, the UK was my first choice because I could practise my midwifery career there in a way that was not open to me in Nigeria. In due course this was the avenue that opened up. I returned to the UK in June 1990 as a dual-qualified person, having the potential for a satisfactory career as a midwifery practitioner.

Midwifery practice in the UK had advanced greatly in the sixteen years since my first visit, with new technology and additional skills, so this move presented a big challenge. I discussed the possibility of relocation and my decision with my brother, who assured me of his continuing advice and support, so I set about the application process joyfully and with peace of mind. All UK-trained midwives who had been absent from the UK for any length of time were required to undergo a three-month return to practice course in a recommended midwifery training school. I applied to many of these from Nigeria, attended interviews in the UK and eventually chose Farnborough Hospital in Kent. Having completed the course there successfully, we were encouraged to apply for jobs in the NHS because there was an acute shortage of midwives in the UK at that time. I applied to Queen Charlotte's (part of Hammersmith Hospital), where I started work on 14 September 1991. At the same time, I was granted a four-year residency in the UK and moved into the nurses' home accommodation on Goldhawk Road.

I liked living in the nurses' home as it was close to my work and good value for money. It was also safe, since the premises had security surveillance. As I settled into my new home and the demanding role at Queen Charlotte's, I was much more relaxed than I had been the last time I came to England. I saw my coming to this country as a progression and a blessing in different aspects of my life. God had spoken to me and lifted me up from the pit. Now His unconditional love and grace kept me going and focused on my job. These built up my confidence, trust and patience. Continual prayer was my bedrock, because no one can do what the Lord did for mankind through Jesus.[2] I looked forward to what He would do in me, through me and with me in the years to come.

---

[2] See John 3:16

CHAPTER THREE

Going Deeper

God had made a gracious promise to me in my hour of need and I decided the time had come to have a proper relationship with Him. The Sunday before I left Nigeria for the UK, I went to a church service. This time my prayer was not out of heartbreak and anguish, but for a different purpose: to establish a relationship with my Creator. I wanted to reciprocate His love, which I had glimpsed when He called me by name and assured me that He would fight for me. This experience had proved to me that the Lord is trustworthy and faithful. I wanted to know more about this God and His ways, so in England I looked for a church where I could become a regular worshipper. I was happy and more enthusiastic than ever before about true worship of the compassionate and loving Father who had spoken to me – a God I had not previously known.

Whilst waiting for my work permit and other official approvals, I rented a converted studio flat in Lewisham for three months. There I went to Sunday worship at St John's Anglican Church on the High Street. I became the custodian of my own life in an entirely new environment, growing in knowledge and understanding of British culture as well as in the practice of my chosen profession, and observing all sorts of unfamiliar lifestyles. When I started work at Queen Charlotte's hospital, I attended a church service once when the hospital management organised a special service on Christmas Day 1991, conducted in the hospital foyer and officiated by the hospital chaplain. I was very happy as it was an echo of my freedom.

I had been baptised as a child and now wanted to affirm my own faith as an adult by getting confirmed as a full member of the Church of

England, so one day I approached the chaplain about this. Sadly, just as I was about to start the preparatory classes, it was announced that he was being transferred. This was a disappointment, but not a significant setback; I knew that I was ready for confirmation whenever another opportunity arose.

From Goldhawk Road there are good transport links to central London and farther afield, with the very popular Shepherd's Bush market nearby selling clothing, household goods and a variety of foreign foodstuffs. Every Sunday I would walk around the neighbourhood looking for a church I could attend, but did not find one. This went on for three months, so during this time I was unable to go to Sunday worship. I always travelled on buses and trains to avoid losing my bearings as I had not yet become familiar with my new surroundings, and one day this led me to the right place.

It was a bright, cold, wintry day. I walked to Sainsbury's supermarket on Chiswick High Road. As I came out of the shop, going towards the bus stop in front of a coffee shop, I spied an old church building on the green across the road. I crossed over to read the information on the notice board and realised the building was still in use. It was called Christ Church, Turnham Green. I suspected this could be the answer to my request for God to place me in a church where I could worship Him in spirit and in truth, but that did not stop me from thinking of objections. The obvious problem was the distance to the church from where I lived.

"How far is it from where you live to the church?" I knew the voice. It was the same one that had spoken to me as I sat weeping on the bedroom floor in Nigeria. "If you wanted to buy something from Marks & Spencer's in Brent Cross, would you consider the distance?"

I was shocked because this was the second time God had spoken to me so clearly. It seemed He was not going to take no for an answer.

Next Sunday morning I did as I was told and came for the first time to a service at Christ Church, which is where God had placed me to worship Him. The congregation was small compared to churches in Nigeria and, to begin with, I was the only black person. That was odd, but I quickly embraced the fact that I was going there for a relationship with God, not people. As time went by, I made this my regular place of worship, though there was no formal introduction or friendly chat afterwards, as there is nowadays. After a while I approached the vicar to discuss the possibility of my being confirmed. He told me that he was going to retire the following month but gave me a handwritten referral to the vicar at a church nearby. After preparatory classes with another member of our congregation (who has been my best friend in the parish ever since), I was finally confirmed in 1993. I was very happy, as my name was included on the church register and electoral roll. It felt like a real step forward in my faith journey – I was no longer just a Sunday Christian; I was a full member of the Church of England.

The following year a new vicar arrived at Christ Church: Rev. James Dainty (popularly known as Jim) and Angela, his lovely wife. Through Jim's sermons, I perceived that something vital was present in my life that I could not identify but I was prepared to receive the full abundance of whatever God had in store for me. Going to church on Sunday mornings made me happy because these sermons had a remarkable impact on me. I was involved in most of the activities in the church and this became a greater part of my life. I felt I was living for God daily, which gave me joy, peace and a sense of belonging.

The sermon one Sunday lit up my heart. Jim preached about the unconditional love of God.[3] He said God loves us irrespective of our sinful nature and forgives all our sins through Jesus Christ His Son. Wow! What an amazing grace, I thought, and wondered why I had not been told this before. I had lived with the wrong perception of God from a tender age because of my strict upbringing. God is not scary; though He does discipline those He loves[4] when they are disobedient. I reflected on this for a whole week.

The following week's sermon was also unbelievable; Jim preached on John 3:16. We were told to memorise it and recited it every Sunday at the beginning of the service for a few weeks. That was a bonus for me: two pieces of Good News in successive weeks. The second revealed to me why we celebrate Good Friday and Easter. How amazing was that! For me, it was like throwing a shot put with a complete lack of enthusiasm but finding it went much farther than expected.

I collected all the study notes and shared the messages with my friends at work. I bought a study bible and started reading it regularly using the Scripture Union Daily Bread Bible reading guide, and prayed all the time. Up until this point I had always talked more about God than Jesus because I perceived God as being higher than His Son –

---

[3] See Ephesians 2:1-10
[4] See Proverbs 3:12

hence the reason I had no personal relationship with Jesus. Now I longed to know more about the incredible three-in-one God. Today, I embrace the Holy Trinity, their impact on my life and their superfluous abundance. The radiance in my heart and soul has helped me a lot in my journey to identify their roles and the meaning of God's Word with clarity. There was so much more to being a Christian that I did not perceive or understand at that time. Now I know how much God loves me, and I love Him with all my heart.

I am now gaining wisdom, knowledge and an understanding of my relationship with Jesus. I am delighted, confident and bold, empowered by the Holy Spirit. Through diligence, hard work and motivation in various skills, I excelled in my career, but the beacon for my faith journey and revelation as a Christian was lit by Jim Dainty and it is something I will remember him for throughout the rest of my life. I was spiritually immature and his sermons built me up. I cannot speak for other people, but I did not know the reason Jesus was crucified until after Jim's sermon on John 3:16, when I came to understand that while I was still a sinner, Jesus died for me.[5] What have I got to boast about, except the fact that Jesus, Son of the Almighty God, is my Lord and personal Saviour? He is alive in my life in joy or sorrow and will always be for me. Is that not the most amazing assurance and insurance?

One of the happiest days in my life was when I was among sixteen members of our congregation commissioned to serve as communion ministers. As I held the chalice in my hands, no one except the Lord can fathom how humble I felt to serve my brothers and sisters with those holy gifts, reaching out to them in the love of Jesus according to His command. I have always seen it as a special privilege. After the three-year term of my ministry expired, I was re-nominated for another three years. What a blessing to be able to serve in this way – but the Lord was by no means finished with me.

---

[5] See Romans 5:8

CHAPTER FOUR

Pilgrimage

In October 1997 the churches in Chiswick organized a trip to Israel. I had a long-standing desire to visit Jerusalem, the city of God, for three very personal reasons.

Pain: excruciating bodily pain. I had experienced deep hurt as a result of my marriage problems, but now it was my body that screamed out in agony. Five years earlier I had slipped and fallen in the rain on the way back from church. My left knee was badly bruised, but what I did not realise at the time was that I had broken a bone in the joint. I suffered agony for years, which got worse in winter. Whilst I did not really know much about Jesus or have a real relationship with Him, I knew that He had the power to heal. If I went to Israel I could not fail to walk in His footsteps, though I may not physically see the footprints. All I needed was to tread the sand He had walked on; that would be enough to heal any illness. What a weird thought that might seem, a throwback to my Nigerian childhood when people placed bibles under the pillows of the sick – but a reality indeed. So this was my first reason for being so keen to visit Israel: I desperately needed divine healing, and thought there was no better place to get it.

The second reason was baptism. I had been baptised as a child, but never as an adult. Going to Israel offered the chance to be immersed in the River Jordan at Yardenit, at the actual spot where Jesus was baptised by John the Baptist. Now that I was beginning to experience the joy of a proper relationship with the Lord, it seemed right that I should affirm my faith in this way.

My third reason is still very personal. Perhaps I will tell that story one day, but not here.

At any rate, expectations were high as our party set foot in the Holy Land for the first time, and my excitement grew as my turn came to be plunged under the waters of the River Jordan – the same water that had touched the skin of Jesus. It was a very reflective and joyful moment. When Jim and Richard Perry, our churchwarden, lifted me back up to the surface, I was at peace but tearful and smiling. It was an incredible mixed feeling of joy and serenity, an experience of a lifetime – but there was more to come.

At Mount Nebo, I held onto the pole on which Moses put up the bronze snake[6] and prayed to be blessed with the gift of prayer. Though I perceived I had the potential for intercession, I asked the Lord to bless me with wisdom and revelation of His power so that I might know and serve Him better in all that I do. I requested His enlightenment in my heart to understand my calling and also to be filled up with a surge of His strength and patience to sustain my faith and be able to channel my supplications through Jesus. My faith then was so little and not dependent on Jesus, but despite this the awesome God knew my heart and worked His purpose out for me according to His will through the Messiah.

When God wants to work out His mystery, He can use any circumstance to fulfil His plans and purposes. He is omnipresent and omnipotent, the beginning and the end. He loves us better than we love ourselves. He is the only one that sees our hearts, and so He engages with us from the inside and not in terms of physical appearance.[7] Whenever we undertake any task, easy or difficult, trusting only in our own strength and understanding without involving Him, it will always turn out disastrous and daunting. This was my experience when I chose to visit the symbolic Nabataean monastery in Petra without the slightest idea of how difficult and tedious it would be to climb 850 steps up the rocky terrain to reach this building. It was every pilgrim's desire to make this trip, yet God knew that I could not do it in my own strength, and so He intervened. The encounter that resulted was the highlight of my pilgrimage. When God calls an individual by name it comes with goodness and His grace – our part is to be patient and faithful, trusting in His incomprehensible power, authority and righteousness.

---

6 See Numbers 21:9
7 See 1 Samuel 16:7

This is how it happened. At Petra, our team leaders gave us two choices: either a tour of the Nabatean village or a three-hour round-trip climbing to the monastery. Seven opted for the second choice and, despite my damaged and painful knee, I was one of them. The briefing was fascinating and the task of getting there intriguing, but was it that easy to accomplish? No!

It was a very hot day; the sky was bright and blue with scorching sunshine. The road to the monastery was very rugged, winding and carved out of the rocks, and the valley ahead looked frightening. Five in our group were very fast but my hotel roommate and I lagged behind because both of us had previous leg injuries. From the start, I was unsure whether I could do it because of my injury, but I was willing to try. Oh dear, what luck! I was clumsy and right at the start I fell on my bad left knee, which bled a lot from nasty-looking grazes.

At that point I was convinced I could not go on, though my roommate tried to encourage me and climbed ahead. It was no longer cowardice but simple good sense to admit defeat and join the village tour. I turned to make my way back to where they were.

"Alaereba! Come up – you can do it!" It was that voice again.

I hesitated because I no longer had the confidence to carry on.

The voice spoke again. "You can do it! Come up, my arms are stretched out to embrace you."

My thought was, this is God calling me, and how can I disobey him? After pausing for a while, I carried on, but those who were returning from the monastery offered only discouragement. When I asked them how far it was from the point I had reached, the answer was always, "A long way off." Then I had some of the villagers who transport pilgrims with their camels asking me to use them as a means of transport. Twice I sat down on the ground lamenting why I had decided to go, but I had come to a point of no return on a very tedious journey, and I had to be obedient to God.

I had started the trip with two cans of coke in my hand. When I fell, I lost one, and I had drunk the second. Now there was nothing else to quench my thirst in the intense sunshine. I must have looked pathetic, albeit hopeful that the end would justify the means.

Though I was tired, I carried on in loneliness until I only had to turn around the edge of a rock to reach the monastery courtyard. At this point I perceived a glimpse of hope and strength – enough to summon up courage for the last leg because I saw some pilgrims resting in this courtyard. I was so frightened standing on the corner of the last high point that I decided to crawl on my bottom until I reached the courtyard safely.

The six other members of our team had arrived long before and were resting, waiting for me to join them. Goodness gracious! The Holy Spirit fell upon me with joy and peace. I was euphoric, singing and praying aloud, pacing from one end of the courtyard to the other. I walked up to the front entrance of the gigantic monastery, though I made no attempt to go inside because peeping through the gap in the door I saw a very dark, huge and frightening space. All I could hear was the echo from the noises of pilgrims as if there were many people inside shouting.

Before long it was time for us to set off back down the mountain, down that steep slope that I had climbed with such difficulty earlier in the day. Oh, what a difference the Spirit of God made! I was as swift as a bird and even helped some of the other team members climb down. They were amazed at my joy and stamina. Some asked what the trick behind my sudden change of outlook and surge of energy was. I told them that I received what was kept for me in the monastery but never spoke to anybody about my encounter with God. They might have thought it was fantasy, though I know the truth. It goes to confirm that, "The fear of the Lord is the beginning of wisdom."[8]

Jesus is a miracle-working God. I can testify from my own experience that He does not change and will never change. One mystery I have experienced in a relationship with Him is this: He does not judge anyone because He knows about all our weaknesses and He is mighty to save everybody, no matter what. He is the Good Shepherd[9] and gives everyone a second chance – an opportunity to make amends. Hence Peter, who denied him, was commissioned to lead and feed His sheep.[10] He called the tax collector Matthew from his booth to follow Him as His disciple.[11] When we seek to have relationship with Him, He will make a way. That was the story of Zacchaeus[12] and a man regarded a 'sinner' received salvation. Saul (Paul), an apostle to the Gentiles,

---

[8] Proverbs 9:10a
[9] See John 10:11-12
[10] See John 21:15-19
[11] See Matthew 9:9
[12] See Luke 19:1-9

appointed by Jesus, had an encounter with the risen Lord[13] on a self-commissioned mission to Damascus to arrest and bring to justice all those who called on the name of Christ. What about me? I had ample opportunity to know Jesus, but paid no attention until He came into my life to rescue me and heal my brokenness. In my encounters with the Messiah, He always took the initiative in all circumstances and situations. That is the good news of Jesus. He is an amazing God!

Returning to England was not the end of my pilgrimage but the continuation of it, as I did my best to walk daily in the ways of God and to be alert to His promptings. One day I came back from work very late and I was in a rush to get to the bank in Chiswick before it closed because I needed some money for the weekend and my debit card was in transit. It was well into Friday afternoon and obvious that, however fast I walked, I would not get there on time. I had no cash on me, so the only option was using my chequebook to make a withdrawal at the counter.

I was frustrated and murmured to myself, "Lord, I wish you would give me money for my bus fare," thinking this would enable me to get to the bank on time.

Instantly, I heard a voice: "Look down in front of you."

I did and there in front of me I found a £10 note!

I was very happy. I did not go to the bank. Instead I went to the supermarket and bought a few things to take me through the weekend. Who can quantify such faithfulness and generosity? No one in the whole universe!

On another occasion, while I was planning an eight-week annual leave to spend Christmas with my family in Nigeria, I suddenly realised I had only a week to renew my passport. I was in a panic. If there is one thing that causes me stress and anxiety, it is going to the Nigerian Embassy on Fleet Street, because of my past experiences there. The truth is, I detest visiting it. I prayed about it for a week and, to be honest, if there had been any way of avoiding the situation, I would have grabbed it. Everyone turns up without an appointment, so there is always a disorderly crowd of people waiting.

It was a cold winter morning; I got there in good time, the queue was building up in front of the embassy and snow was falling. Without a valid passport I could not book a flight. As the door opened to let us

---

[13] See Acts 9

in, we struggled to get through in an orderly manner. My faith was tested and I was angry, though I tried my hardest to be civil. I had no idea Jesus was saying to me, "You of little faith, why are you so afraid?"[14]

I had a miracle! Among the crowd I heard my African name "Alaereba". I turned around and there was my second cousin, a senior member of staff. The last time we had spoken she had told me she had been posted to the Nigerian embassy in Zaire. I did not know about her transfer to London. She took me straight to the passport office and within an hour we completed the formalities and I was told to come back for my new passport in two weeks. It might seem unfair to the other people who were waiting that I received this preferential treatment, but I have a supernatural power that takes care of all my affairs, and this was proof.

As the appointed date to collect the passport drew close, I imagined facing some difficulties because my cousin had told me she would be on holiday then. I was worried, so the night before I rang up a staff member I knew vaguely to ask for their help. Then, as I was praying the next morning, the Lord challenged me: "You have given this job to me. Who else do you want to help?" In truth, the difficulty and hassle in that embassy are such that even if a pastor went there for the same purpose, he or she would seek help!

At the passport office, I was determined to do whatever it took to get through the door. As I struggled to get in, the doorman stopped me from going through but allowed others to pass. In anger, I screamed at him.

Then the unexpected happened. A female voice called my name. "Alaereba, have you not collected your passport?" Then an order was passed: "Allow her to go through. She is my sister." The next command was, "Come, let's take the lift."

Wow! All that was going through my brain was, "Who is this angel from God?" My cousin was on holiday. Who, then, was this nice lady? I could not work it out. My memory went blank; I did not recognize her and was embarrassed to ask who she was. She was doing most of the talking from the moment we entered the lift till we got into her office. My responses were yes or no as I did not want to embarrass myself or make her angry for not recognizing my own flesh and blood.

---

[14] Matthew 8:26

As we sat down, she called a clerk and gave him my details to collect my passport from the head of the passport office. Meanwhile, she was sharing family news that I was not yet aware of without realizing that I did not recognize her or remember her name. Jesus Christ utterly took control of the job I gave to him until it was accomplished.

About an hour later the clerk came back and handed my new passport to his boss. The moment she handed my passport over to me the Lord revealed her identity to me. She was my cousin Bekinwari – we even share the same surname. She had come back from holiday a week early and returned to work that same day. I am never shy to tell people about Jesus and this was an appropriate moment. I told her all about His intervention in my passport renewal, gave her a small wooden cross I always carried in my handbag, and told her to trust Jesus all the time no matter the circumstance because He is the one in control of our lives.

I had taken time off from my job to go to the embassy that morning. When I returned to work, I told my colleagues what had happened. The following day one of them gave me a British Airways voucher offering discount flights to Africa for visits of a fortnight or longer. With that I received a £100 discount from my very expensive December fare because most airlines were fully booked. Hitherto, I had played the National Lottery and won £20 only once. Through the incidents of that week I learnt a very valuable lesson: that I did not need to bet, for God can provide all my needs. He is my security, not money I may never win from petty gambling.

This was not the only practical example of how God looked after me at this time. In August 1999, Jesus shut the lens of the CCTV camera in a shop to take away the embarrassment and shame of shoplifting from me. He knew I was absent-minded and innocent and that I was not a thief. On a hot summer's day, I went shopping to buy presents in the sales as I was planning to go home on holiday. I had an invitation to attend a colleague's wedding reception that evening, too. At the shop I paid for the items I wanted but then left the shop still carrying one of the other unwanted items, complete with its hanger and security tag! As I was walking to the bus stop, I heard a voice prompting me to look at my hand. I had no idea why, until I looked and saw myself holding the briefs. I checked the rest of the items in all the bags and found a similar pair to the one I was holding. I panicked and felt as if my blood circulation would stop.

My first thought was to dump the briefs in the litter bin at the bus stop. Then the voice said to me, "If you dump them in the bin, you have stolen them. Take them back to the shop." Yes, it appeared as if I was free and safe beyond the four walls of the shop but I was feeling guilty of stealing already. It was as though two powerful forces were pulling me apart; Jesus telling me to return the briefs to the store to be free from stealing under His protection and Satan telling me that I would be caught if I went back into the shop.

Nevertheless, I went back in obedience to my Lord, the item in my hand exposed for all to see. Once again the alarm was not activated, just as it had failed to go off when I first walked out of the shop. All the same, I lost my composure completely, standing on the shop floor looking for either a manager or supervisor to explain what I had done. Amazingly I could not find one. Then I had the prompting for a third time, "Are you stupid? Drop it where you picked it up from and go home."

Though I was set free and there was nothing to incriminate me, I was shaken. My freedom and liberation from this horrible incident were a result of what Jesus did for me on the cross – salvation from sinfulness when He washed me immaculate with His own precious blood and said, "It is finished."[15] He covered the lens in the CCTV camera, proving man's technology powerless before my master planner.

The following day I phoned our vicar and made an appointment to see him. I told him everything that had happened. He must have noticed how frightened I was. He prayed for me and said that if I was caught, convicted and prosecuted, he would stand by me in the court of law to prove my innocence of committing such a crime. That assurance gave me joy and peace of mind. I cannot imagine how I would have lived with such a shame on my family, church, friends and clients.

Anybody who does not walk or have a loving relationship with the "Vine"[16] will have no true testimonies to give; because of that I now count my blessings and no longer pay heed to sorrows. This is not because I do not have any problems. I do, like everyone else, but I believe and trust the awesome power of my only port of call where all my problems are solved, and that makes the difference. I always find refuge and solace in my Lord – and I have never been disappointed, for

---

[15] See John 19:30
[16] See John 15

He knows who I am. He calls me by my name and I am familiar with His voice. Man may judge people for their skin colour, social status or physical appearance, but the Lord looks at the heart.[17] When we are committed to walk with Him, we must trust, obey and act according to His word. Our wisdom depends on the fear of the Lord.[18] Time and again He went before me and took care of me, though naturally I still had much to learn.

---

[17] 1 Samuel 16:7
[18] See Proverbs 9:10

CHAPTER FIVE

Discipline and Provision

Gambling does not necessarily only concern money. It can involve anything that is valuable in life such as health, profession and personal attributes, to name just a few. In naivety I gambled with my own career, which could have had fatal results for my practice. I am a sensitive, cheerful and caring person but also very cautious of my integrity. The story that follows demonstrates God's love, compassion, faithfulness and grace. I learnt a valuable lesson and was thankful to my Father for His discipline. The lesson I take is that gambling, either with or without money, is not an acceptable way of life for those who truly want to follow Jesus.

One day in 2001, I was working on the morning shift on the delivery suite at Queen Charlotte's and took over the care of a woman who had been in labour all night. The woman was about to give birth and as the midwife who had been looking after her on the night shift handed over to me, she joked, "I have done the difficult part all night; you have come in to take over the best part of the birth." I gave her a friendly hug and, in response to what she had said, I held her hands as if we were making an exchange from one to the other. I did not know I had swapped my God-given talent and expertise with that of my friend.

It was a thoughtless gesture and an error of judgment on my part. I helped the woman to a safe, normal birth but from that point onwards almost all my subsequent cases were complicated in one way or the other, until I nearly lost a mother. She gave birth safely but bled excessively afterwards. Despite following all the normal procedures, I could not stop the bleeding. I called for medical assistance, the doctors arrived instantly and I handed over care to them.

I was very distraught, emotionally drained and was thinking, "What a nightmare!" As she was being revived, I moved to the window in the room, looked up and in my thoughts asked God, "Lord, what do you intend to do with me and where did I go wrong?"

It was a miserable week. My colleagues were all very supportive, but none of us could understand the decline in my competence. I prayed tirelessly and fasted, asking God to have mercy on me and to take control of my situation.

The following week, as I was praying, the Lord said to me, "Did you not know that I have blessed your hands for this work? But you have passed your favour over to someone else." That was His discipline for my mistake. Then, in His great mercy and mighty power, the incomprehensible and holy God ended my nightmare, giving me back my skill without loss of life or further mishap. My faithful, loving and compassionate Father turned my sorrow to joy, enabling me to smile again in His grace as a one-to-one (caseload) midwife until my retirement ten years later.

I cannot claim to have a super faith in Jesus Christ, far from it. Yet experience is the best teacher, they say. My relationship with Jesus is based mainly on trusting who He says He is and also my personal experiences through all the encounters I have had with Him. These spur me to worship and acknowledge Him, the Son of God, who has been given "all authority in heaven and on earth" (Matthew 28:18). What has sustained me in my faith journey from the moment Jesus came into my life are trust, obedience and confidence, for He knows and sees the heart. I am always optimistic because whatever He says, He will do, according to the Father's will and His timing. Doubt is a hindrance and an obstacle. My antidote to it is prayer because God is very much involved in all our conversations with Him and, "What is impossible with men is possible with God."[19]

Another challenge at work arose that same year in relation to accommodation, and here God provided for me in the most beautiful way. Safety and proximity to my place of work have always been priorities in my choice of where to live, which is why I had stayed in the nurses' home on Goldhawk Road for nine years. Now, the hospital trust decided that these premises were to be put up for sale, causing problems for a large number of the staff living there, who had nowhere

---

[19] Luke 18:27

else to go. The situation was difficult for both the staff and the management. There was mass exodus of staff to other places where accommodation was easier to come by. I was in a dilemma. I loved my job and practice but found it difficult to find suitable accommodation.

We were served the final notice to vacate the nurses' home by the first week of December 2001. As I came home from work after an early shift on my last Friday in the building, rain was falling. My belongings were packed in boxes provided by the management but I had nowhere to send them. Looking through my window at the dripping trees outside, I called out to God. Though He knew I would become homeless, in humility I said to him, "Lord, almost everyone has left their room. I am still here because I have nowhere to go. If You want me to sit in the rain to continue serving Your people, I am very happy to do so. But Lord, if it is Your will, please give me a place of my own, because for nine years I have lived in this shared space." It was not a prayer but a complaint to my daddy, who knew my situation much better than I did.

As I went to church on Sunday two days later, I was unaware that there was a special service to focus on homelessness. It was in response to the call by a national charity for all churches in the UK to come together as one in prayer to take action against this scandal. I picked up one of their cards distributed on all the seats and prayed the beautiful prayer that was written by Sarah Beresford entitled, "Spotlight on Homelessness". This prayer was a bonus because I saw myself as a desperate and homeless person – though I might have known that God in His mercy was on the case.

On Monday when I went to work, I was told that our management had arranged with a local housing association for us to be put in one of their properties within walking distance of the hospital for the next year, with an option to renew for a further six months. Though the rent was more than we had been paying, the hospital made up the balance. I was given a large bedsit with kitchen and toilet and a big balcony where I kept my pot plants. Amazingly, the incomprehensible God had given me exactly what I had asked for. More than that, through the government's key worker scheme I was eventually able to buy a one-bedroom flat of my own. Truly, His provision for me has been incredible!

God was teaching me more and more about His character and trustworthiness, but He was also leading me onwards in the Christian life. I was about to learn a valuable lesson in patience. We all take risks daily without necessarily considering the consequences and, though we often get away with it, sometimes our luck fails.

One common risk is running for a bus instead of waiting for the next one to come along. As the wise saying goes, better safe than sorry. In June 2002, I was not wise. As I ran I tripped on an uneven pavement, breaking my right wrist and forearm. The bus driver saw the accident but drove off, though two women passing by stopped to help me back to my feet. One of them stayed with me while I tried to call an ambulance, but half an hour later there was still no response and I was becoming desperate. Having broken the same wrist twelve years beforehand, I feared the worst and the pain was intense.

Just then, the lady who was helping me said that a driver waiting at the nearby traffic lights was trying to attract my attention. When I turned around, he called my name and said to me, "Come over here. What have done to your hand?" It was the minicab driver who had moved my belongings from the nurses' home to temporary accommodation at my cousin's family home in West Ealing.

Though he had someone in his minicab, he took me along, too, dropping the other passenger at her destination and then taking me to the hospital. It was a good job he did, since there was still no sign of an ambulance.

After the minicab driver dropped me at the hospital he offered to go and inform my cousin and her husband and, if possible, bring one of them to the hospital to see to my needs. Not only did he do that, but he came back at my request at half past two in the morning to take my cousin's husband from Charing Cross Hospital to home for work in the morning.

I regard the unexpected appearance of this driver at the scene and his subsequent kindness as a mystery of Almighty God's provision, since the national safety and emergency services that I was supposed to rely on failed me. The Sovereign Lord was in total control the moment I fell down. It was through His grace that those two women were at the scene of the accident to help me and He caused one to stay behind to support and comfort me. Finally, He brought the minicab driver to provide the transportation that took me to hospital. This is an authentic proof that our God is alive, mighty to save, has total control of all our situations and continues to move in mysterious ways in each individual life. It was as well that I was in the care of such a wonderful God, for once again there were testing times ahead.

Chapter Six

Blindness

The text in front of me was a complete blur. I could not make out a single letter, not even the biggest ones. I was going blind. For years I had been having problems with my vision and had gone for regular eye tests, only to be told that there was nothing seriously wrong and I just needed more powerful lenses. Supposedly skilled opticians had failed to correctly diagnose the problem in my right eye despite my persistent complaints of diminishing vision each time I went to see them. As the years went by, the problems grew worse.

I started having severe pain, the eyes were gritty and weepy, and though I asked the opticians to refer me to Moorfields Eye Hospital for a second opinion, they refused. Instead, they prescribed another pair of glasses, which I bought out of desperation. I went back the following weekend and was promised a referral to my GP, but again this did not happen. At a third visit I pressed them to give me a handwritten referral to submit at my GP surgery. This time I refused to accept further delay because I could hardly see moving objects until they were very close and when my eyes were tested I could no longer read the letters.

Disappointingly, I received the same uncaring attitude from my GP when I went to deliver the letter. He also refused to refer me to the Moorfields Eye Hospital and though he promised to refer me to a new eye unit at Central Middlesex Hospital, he did not. Within a week my vision deteriorated yet further and I was becoming desperate. I went back to the doctors again, where I saw a locum GP.

He was not able to make a referral to Moorfields, but he told me that there was an accident and emergency department there and hinted that I should go. I am grateful to him because without his hint I would have lost the remaining twenty-five percent of vision left in my right eye. After a series of tests at Moorfields I was diagnosed with having congested bilateral cataracts and acute open-angle glaucoma in my right eye. I had lost three-quarters of the vision in that eye, so I was partially blind – this as a result of the opticians' negligence and my GP's failure to act on my concerns. Over the course of six or seven years I had believed the opticians' test results. After all, it was not my profession and not my place to challenge their professional integrity, competence and practice. In that space of time they prescribed three pairs of glasses for me to buy from them.

At Moorfields I was put under the care of the glaucoma clinic and started treatment to reduce the very high intra-ocular pressure in my eye. I was also given three weeks' sick leave until further review. At a subsequent review in the glaucoma clinic, the pressure in the right eye improved, no further damage was detected in that eye and I was booked for a cataract operation in the left eye, where the intra-ocular pressure was normal. I was discharged from sick leave and returned to work, which was a big relief.

A critical reader will notice that I enjoyed the walk with Jesus and all He was doing in my life. My changing perception of His persona and the reasons for making a trip to Israel show the progress I was making in my faith walk, but up to that point I had not made a declaration to Jesus as my personal Saviour and Lord of my life. Human beings always take important things for granted and that is exactly what I did until I nearly lost all the vision in my right eye. I am lucky that Jesus is a loving, patient, compassionate and faithful Messiah who understands His own. I was unsure of the reason for His delay in healing my sight, and was upset that He did not do for me as He had done for blind Bartimaeus.[20]

My hope of a healing miracle diminished daily. I was unable to read the Bible and did not know what else to do. At that point Jesus intervened and dictated a prayer to me that I wrote down, word for word, headed, "The Peace of God be with you."

> *God is Peace*
> *He has given us Peace*
> *He wants us to love Peace*

---

[20] See Mark 10:46-52

Through him we perceive Peace
He wants us to share Peace
We have received Peace
Having Jesus is Peace
He wants us to live in Peace
May God's Peace shine through you. Amen.

When we make our supplications under stress we may not make relevant requests but Jesus, who knows us better than we know ourselves, will provide our needs. He knew I required spiritual and physical healing. Therefore, He tackled what He saw as the priority, providing spiritual wellbeing to keep my body and soul together before further intervention. On reflection I realised that I needed this prayer more than anything else and continued to use it till I was started on the right medication for my eyes. My underlying fear was not only not being able to return to work, but the ability to cope with blindness. The prince of peace sustained my progress in this prayer and the medical treatment until, in early 2003, the time came for the cataract operation on my left eye.

I was still uncertain how to cope with blindness and this was a worry as I was being taken to the operating theatre in a wheelchair. That whole morning all I did was recite Psalm 23, right up to the point when local anaesthetic was administered and an incision was made into my left eyeball.

As I was lying still on the operating table my thoughts wandered. In my fright, I silently asked, "Where is Jesus when all these things are happening to me?"

The right eye was covered, so obviously I could not see anything, but I perceived a tall and slim man leaning on his right side against a door on my left. He walked up to me, took my left hand clenched in his and said, "That is why I am here to support you."

With this, I kept my hand in a fist till the surgery was over and I was transferred to the recovery room. When I was ready to be taken back to the day ward the man let go of my hand and left.

From that day, I had the feeling that Jesus was always with me in the theatre during each of my eight eye operations, and clenched my fist throughout as I had done the first time. My courage, patience, perseverance, strength and hope came through Him.

God continues to love us so dearly irrespective of whatever we have done in the past, and that love is above everything that we pursue in our own strength.[21] Indeed, He is the way, the truth and the life.[22] I am happy and grateful to the Lord, despite living with partial blindness in one eye; my ability to perform in all areas of life has not diminished or been impaired in any way. It is thirteen years since I was diagnosed with glaucoma, an incurable condition that can cause blindness. The treatment for glaucoma does not restore lost vision but merely controls the high intra-ocular pressure so as to prevent further damage. I count myself lucky because, despite the difficulty in controlling the unstable pressures in both eyes, there was no further damage and my sight is good using intra-ocular lenses. The power of the Holy Trinity has been upon me to sustain my health in abundance throughout my career till my retirement in 2011. I had eight eye operations, both major and minor, in conjunction with using glaucoma eye drops and ointments, but I cannot complain when I see other cases whose vision appears worse than mine. Instead, I glorify the Father in heaven.

Comparing suffering from glaucoma to my experience with the side effects of the medication, it is very difficult to say which is worse. With the exception of steroids and antibiotics, all my medication contains preservatives. I am allergic to these and over time they give me acute breathing problems.

The reactions I suffered varied from red, itchy eyes to dry skin with persistent respiratory problems. On a few occasions, I complained about the medication, but though it was changed, all conventional glaucoma eye drops contain preservatives to ensure they retain their effectiveness. The stronger the medication was, the worse the side effects became and I thought I had only two options: either to continue to suffer from the prevailing wheezing insomnia and breathlessness using the medication or stop treatment and become blind. The former was my preference though my breathing was increasingly difficult and I was listless due to insufficient oxygen saturation in my bloodstream. The thought of having an eighth operation, booked for 14 May 2015, was scary because it involved an implant in the partially blind right eye under general anesthetic to improve drainage. Having developed full-blown asthma, I went to see my GP, who tested my peak flow (lung

---

[21] See Romans 8:37-39
[22] See John 14:6

capacity oxygen). It was barely at normal volume, so he prescribed a ventolin inhaler to help me breathe better and improve the oxygen capacity in my bloodstream. This worked for a short period, but as time went by I became worse, even at rest. In addition, I developed a persistent non-productive cough. I was scared at night as I was unable to sleep, despite propping myself up in bed using four pillows and some cushions, and I was still restless and gasping for breath. For two years I put off having the operation and became more and more scared by the persistent and severe asthma attacks.

By March 2015, I could not walk long distances without taking a rest. I stopped complaining about it to the doctors because changing the prescription was not helpful. It appeared as if I had no other choice than to carry on suffering.

What kept me going was the thought that Jesus was always lying beside me in my bed and I talked to Him a lot for comfort. On two occasions, I wanted to call the paramedics to take me to the nearest hospital to be given oxygen, but on second thoughts, I said to Jesus, "How can I go to the hospital while you are here lying beside me?"

The first time this happened, He said to me, "Remove the cross on your neck and place it on your chest."

I responded and secured it on my nightgown with a safety pin. Less than half an hour later I felt better and slept till nine in the morning.

Then on the second occasion I made the same plea. This time He said, "Turn on to your left side and face the big cross." (I have a big tapestry cross in a corner beside my bed, a present from one of my friends that I cherish greatly.)

I did as I was told, and again had a long, restful sleep. It was the Lord's strength that enabled me to go through that period of fear and anxiety; otherwise I could not have coped.

During prayers at Christ Church three weeks before my planned operation, I heard a prompting to ask one of the teenage boys to pray for me because of my concerns for the operation. At first I felt embarrassed because I seldom spoke to this boy, though I had known him as a baby. But hearing the voice a second time, I gave in and asked him after the service to pray for me. We went to the chancel because it was peaceful and quiet there. I told him about my vision and the prompting.

When I went to the hospital the following week before the operation, the pressure in both eyes was normal and I was no longer afraid of the surgery. As scheduled, on the morning of the operation I was admitted onto the day ward for routine pre-operative procedures and assessment. When the consultant surgeon and anesthetist came to see me, I politely told them that I would not have the operation under general anesthetic, explaining my reasons and concerns. I told them categorically that I would suffer a respiratory arrest on the operating table if I were given general anaesthetic because the severe breathlessness and dry skin that were being caused by my medication suggested that my oxygen saturation was lower than normal. The pre-operative assessments were within normal limits but in the theatre when my oxygen saturation level was monitored it was indeed much lower than the norm. Possibly the doctors took that into account when considering my refusal to have general anaesthetic for a surgical procedure that was estimated to last two hour hours. In the event, I was given oxygen via nasal prongs and had the surgery done under local anaesthetic. The following day I was discharged home with more medication, including another new prescription.

Living in a culture where people do not interact with one another as easily as we do at home in Nigeria, I found it difficult to tell people I knew how ill I was. Surprisingly, nobody noticed, as I felt I had no choice but to put on my usual bright countenance and carry on with life as if all was well. I found this very disappointing, particularly when I contrasted it with how Africans take care of their kith and kin regardless of any previous friendships or relationships. Knowing how different things are in Britain, I try to cope on my own with any situations I find myself in and not expect much from community or society generally. This is the reason I cannot keep a distance from Jesus: having Him in my life makes a world of difference. He will always be my confidant, comforter, companion and my first port of call in prayers.

The new medication I was given on discharge from the hospital caused me more harm than good. In June 2015, I went to the hospital for routine post-operative review. The Holy Spirit empowered me to speak my mind to the doctor who saw me that day about the new medication I had been prescribed, and I took it along with the intention of telling the doctor that I was not going to use that particular eye drop any more. I regard that doctor as one sent to me by the Almighty and Sovereign Lord. As I was called into the consulting room I told the doctor politely that I was not going to use the new eye drops again. The doctor asked why I was using medication that contains preservatives when it was clearly documented in my hospital file that I am allergic to preservatives, and she said there was preservative-free glaucoma medication in stock in the hospital pharmacy. She then took my notes to confer with the consultant and reported my complaint to him. When she returned, she announced the good news that all my medication was discontinued, and the one she recommended was prescribed instead. I started using the new medication in the clinic that very day and within forty-eight hours of using the new eye drops I noticed a remarkable improvement in my respiratory symptoms.

I am partially blind in my right eye, have screws and plates in my right forearm and unstable intra-ocular pressures in both eyes, yet the gracious, faithful and mysterious God has kept me safe and healthy without any adverse effects from any of these things. In this way, He enabled me to carry on working in the vocation where He had called me to serve Him and to provide expectant mothers with excellent professional care. My expertise as a midwife spoke for itself in my one-to-one (caseload) practice. I fulfilled my vision as a midwife – motivated, experienced and possessed of amazing skills, and enjoying momentous job satisfaction. I have the rare opportunity of seeing some of the mums I worked with and their children whom I helped deliver safely. That is the greatest joy I cherish in my life and the Holy Trinity made all of that possible.

CHAPTER SEVEN

Bereavement

There was an idol in my life and I did not know it. On 11 September 2009, my brother died following a brief illness, at a point when my new-found faith was still young. His passing threw everything into chaos and the thought of arranging his funeral was my worst nightmare. It seemed as if the wick in my kerosene lamp was snipped off. My gradually transforming life with Jesus disintegrated. I was saddened, downcast and inconsolable, confronted by the painful confirmation that I was completely alone in the world. My brother and I used to telephone each other every day, so it was like a bad dream the following morning when I dialled his number and it kept ringing without reply. It was only then I remembered he had died the previous day. Who can solve that type of disorientation? I telephoned my manager at work and told her what had happened. I was given a week's compassionate leave and four weeks' annual leave to travel to Nigeria to arrange his funeral and burial. I was plunged into acute depression and would not believe he was dead until I saw his body in the mortuary. Pain threw me into a gloomy pit filled with fear and stress. I appeared to be composed outwardly but internally I was in disarray, lost my self-esteem and became trapped in my own anguish.

In my imagination, holding onto the tassels of Jesus' garment for sanity and strength was not secure enough, so I went into His pouch so that He could carry me along as a kangaroo carries its young – in this way I would be able to give my beloved brother a send-off that his caring and gentle life deserved, irrespective of my sadness. After the funeral I could not face life without him and the idea of returning to London so broken with such low self-esteem frightened me the more. I was overwhelmed by the reaction of my clients when I told them the reason for an unplanned trip to Nigeria because I had to make adequate arrangements for their follow-up care in my absence. I did not allow my personal loss and pain to jeopardise either them or their unborn babies' care and well-being, but all the same I was broken inside.

My brother's death was obviously a great loss and pain to the entire family, but mine was unbearable. He was not just a brother but a friend, soulful confidant and role model. I have half-siblings and other relatives but the love in those relationships is not the same as I had with my brother. We were orphans together and very close. We had the same upbringing and shared many similar values. We always lived together, cared for and protected each other's interests from a tender age. The only time we lived apart was in pursuit of our careers. He went to the United States of America to study petroleum engineering at the University of Oklahoma while I came to the UK for my midwifery education and practice. Both of us returned home into lucrative jobs until he retired and we were both looking forward to my own retirement in April 2011.

When Jesus intervened two months after the loss, He did not give me any option or chance for second thoughts because He knew how and what I felt. The most uncomfortable situation I found was being trapped in my own pain and despair without seeking help. Openness would not only have been a better approach for that particular moment, but would also have offered hope of future recovery, yet it took me a long time to accept the reality because my brother and I had had such a unique bond. My healing process would have been faster but I refused to let go of my gloom, which made me to realize how much I idolised my brother.

My brokenness and darkness were unbearable. Bereavement caused great pain and loneliness. People react differently in similar situations, and I wished I knew an easier way to tackle it. Unfortunately, there was none because I did not have the emotional capacity to handle it. My very new faith and transformation went down the drain completely because I did not know of anyone who could love me as my brother did. The fact that I am writing about it now without tears in my eyes is a mystery, and my gratitude to God shows how much Jesus impacted my life in this time of darkness and gloom.

Whenever I read the Bible I felt reassured that I have Jesus to turn to at all times. That was how I had treated my brother when he was alive;

I saw him as my rock. Now I recognised that the hope, comfort, joy and peace I received from Jesus were the sources of my healing and that His love endures forever.[23] I could not fathom how much Jesus loves me till He came into my life when I was grieving for my brother. In November 2009, two months after my brother's passing, I heard a voice as close to me as if the speaker were standing next to me. It said, "You always said your brother loved you. If you thought your brother loved you, I love you more than your brother did. The things I can do for you, your brother could not do for you."

I felt shocked, as if I had received a blow to my face. I wept uncontrollably but I dared not start any open confrontation because I knew it was not the voice of a man but that of a supernatural being.

In my mind, I thought, "Well then, I would love to see what you can do for me that my brother could not…"

Instantly, I had a strange feeling and saw a bright cloud in front of me, like thin fog. I sensed a surge of energy within me and was able to look at the image where the voice came from.

The following Sunday, I met a friend in Christ Church before the start of the service. We exchanged greetings as usual and she said to me, "I have not seen you for a couple of weeks."

I told her about my loss and my trip to Nigeria for my brother's funeral.

All of a sudden I heard a prompting as if coming from the ceiling above my head that twice insisted, "Tell her the truth."

Reluctantly I said, "It seemed as if I loved my brother more than God." Embarrassed, I went back to my seat and sobbed during the service, though nobody took any notice of me.

By January 2010, I felt better as my relationship with Jesus gave me hope for a brighter future. I felt revived from my low self-esteem and that gave me the incentive to plan and organise a thanksgiving celebration service for God's grace and as a memorial on behalf of my beloved brother to mark the first anniversary of his death. I planned this, not as show of affluence, but to bring closure and provide a way forward in my new experience of love in Jesus. My resources were God's providence.

The event was planned for Saturday, 11 September 2010, exactly one year after my brother had died, in our family church in Nigeria. I

---

[23] See Ezra 3:11

chose his favourite songs from the ancient and modern hymn book that is used locally, and the preacher was also my choice, a retired canon of the Anglican church and his close friend.

Throughout the planning, one thing that I considered most was the weather. Nigerian weather can be predicted, unlike in Britain. We have two distinct seasons, rainy and dry, and rain was my biggest concern, as the venue for the reception was to be outside in our courtyard, which was spacious enough to accommodate all the invited guests at the reception, plus any who turned up uninvited. The rainy season starts at about the end of March, with the high point in June and July and an August break with occasional showers in September. Then the dry season gets into full swing with intense sunshine and high temperatures. However, I was hoping for good weather with lots of sunshine and warmth in the middle of September 2010. For the two days immediately preceding the event, there was a heavy tropical downpour. I did not despair, but hoped for better weather the next day, by the grace of the incomprehensible and compassionate God. When I woke up that Saturday morning, the rain had stopped in the night and the sun was shining, the atmosphere was warm and the sky was blue. Wow! It was good and I was euphoric.

Our family members, friends and well-wishers gathered together to decorate the reception venue. Four marquees were put up and festooned with flowers, ribbons and balloons. I expected about five hundred guests, counting both children and adults, since the reception was to be in the open, which meant that anyone could come and have something to eat, according to the local custom. It was such a happy atmosphere with melodious background music of worship, and songs in our dialect and pidgin English. Relatives could not wait to show off their new outfits for the occasion as every detail of the celebration was recorded on a DVD. It was a typical Nigerian memorial for a breadwinner and the head of a respected family.

There was nothing left to be done. The caterer arrived with her staff and the food, to be supervised by nominated relatives. The rest of us went to the church, where the service was to start at 11.00 am. The songs, Gospel reading and Psalms were interspersed with worship songs in English and Nigerian. The youth worship team filled the air with the melody of the organ and local musical instruments. It was the sound of music and dancing to worship the amazing and awesome God, who had showered His love on me and made His very intimate presence known to me in my pain, when I had desperately needed healing and companionship.

When God told Abraham at one hundred and Sarah at ninety years old respectively that they would have a child,[24] the patriarch did not say, "Wow, that sounds good," nor did he say, "Says who?" because he knew God is faithful. I trusted God when He said He would fight my fights for me. My fights are not physical; they encompass any hindrance to my peace and joy. He has continued to fight for me through very difficult circumstances, not least various illnesses, so I have no reason not to trust Him.

As the canon went to the pulpit to preach, the unexpected happened: a thunderstorm broke. I focused on the stormy showers, my thoughts flitting from one possible course of action to another, since the outdoor reception was still to come.

As I was concentrating, looking at the showers, in a trance, I saw a man of average height and build, dressed in white, walking towards me. He tapped on my right shoulder and said, "Kneel down and pray."

I knelt down without hesitation but was lost for words. I thanked God for His providence and accepted the pouring rain as His blessing, acknowledging that nobody had the power to stop the rain for the reception other than Him, and proclaiming that the day's celebration was intended for His praise and grace. I had nothing else to say but kept repeating the same thing over and over again.

The man was still standing beside me listening to my conversation with the Almighty God. Then he spoke to me again. "Remind God that He said, 'Ask and it will be given to you; seek and you will find; knock and the door will be opened to you.'"[25]

I repeated everything after him word for word. Then, as I said amen, I was relieved of my anxiety and worry because the words gave me a ray of hope. I sat back on my seat and the man disappeared. I turned to the pulpit and concentrated on the lengthy sermon.

The congregation listened attentively as the canon recounted his personal experience of his friend, his perception of the deceased's faith in the Trinity, his integrity, kindness and the evidence of God's love and grace in his life. He concluded the sermon with a popular worship song in English, "He's alive again, he's alive. Jesus is alive, forever is alive.

---

[24] See Genesis 17

[25] Matthew 7:7

Amen." The congregation, organist and youth fellowship joined in with local instruments and it was good praise and adoration to the King above all kings. As the canon stepped down from the pulpit the rain stopped abruptly followed by warm weather with intense sunshine. I was euphoric at the faithfulness and grace of our Jehovah Jireh. After the general offering, the family and the congregation sang and danced their way to the chancel to offer their special thanksgiving and prayers for the family. The choir and youth fellowship filled the air with a popular song which reflected what had just happened with the stopping of the rain: "He's a miracle-working God, he's a miracle-working God. Alleluia! He's the Alpha and Omega. God is a miracle-working God. Alleluia!"

Before the dismissal hymn it was announced that the whole congregation was invited to the reception for a final goodbye to the deceased. Every detail of that day was perfect, its simplicity and humility a mirror of my brother's lifestyle. The guests were happy with the attention given to them, including those who only came as a result of the announcement at the church. It was dance, dance and dance in the middle of feasting, a great day of successful celebration and a day I will always remember for the rest of my life. My joy and happiness were akin to the celebration of King David, "while he and the entire house of Israel brought up the Ark of the Lord from the house of Orbed-Edom the Gittite to the City of David".[26] I was filled with joy as Jesus had continued to prove to me that His love for me has no comparison, and for that reason I named September 11, 2010, "The Lord's Day" in the history of our family to tell them about the love, faithfulness and goodness of our gracious Jesus who remains a miracle-working Lord and does not change.

The rain started with a drizzle at about 6 pm, as the guests dispersed, and later turned into a storm that lasted until the following day.

Following my brother's memorial service, my frame of mind gradually improved, I had a more positive outlook and saw each day as a new beginning. I turned fully to Jesus at this point and felt I was in His presence continually. I have been happy since then and not a day goes by without smiles on my face and my being full of joy and happiness. This was a watershed in my life and the lessons I have learnt

---

[26] 2 Samuel 6:14-15

key ones in my relationship with Jesus. He loves us so much that He accepted His Father's will – to die on the cross on our behalf. He wanted me to come clean about something I was struggling with before my brother died. He likes us to be truthful, for He is the Truth. I do not have divided loyalties any more; I am all for Jesus in body, soul and spirit, and He is mine too. I love Him with all that I am, but He loves me more than I can fathom.

As I look back on what I have written in this chapter, I see how through grief and bereavement I gained much experience holding on to the Holy God, believing in Jesus with my immature faith. I learnt much through my brother's death that hitherto I had taken for granted. I survived brokenness and darkness in the light of Jesus. When the unexpected happens, people ask, "Where was God when all this was going on?" Today if I am asked the same question my answer will be, "Do not look back. Move forward and focus on Jesus in prayer to dispel the encircling gloom," – advice and encouragement that holds good in any daunting circumstance. I am still plodding on in my faith journey, protected and secure in the Lord. The grace and peace of God are found in none other than the Prince of Peace. I have discovered this in my relationship with Jesus and He is the true anchor of life, not man. Only He can move mountains and is mighty to save.

CHAPTER EIGHT

Challenge and Attack

God will never betray our trust in Him. He loves us so much that He gave us what is most precious to Him (His Son) to die on our behalf for our own sinfulness. The popular quotation from John 3:16[27] is the affirmation from a loving God. In the same way God said, "So do not fear, for I am with you; do not be dismayed, for I am your God."[28] Wow! From the moment I gave my life to Jesus as Lord and my personal Saviour, I had no more fear because now my focus is on Him. If I am confronted with injustice, my Yahweh will fight to set me free, and if I am in the wrong, by the same token He will discipline me. I was to learn more about His protection and provision in August 2010 when my employment was wrongfully terminated, verbally and unofficially, though there was no fault on my part.

Before I visited Nigeria for my brother's memorial service, I applied for the six weeks' annual leave I would need in March 2010 for the trip. Normally the approval for this would come through within a week if there was reasonable staff coverage on the duty roster. For the first time, I experienced a delay, and after five months had passed I went to find out why approval had not been given. There and then the "bombshell" was dropped. The manager told me that I was not entitled to six weeks' annual leave because I was not going to work as long as I had expected, and would have no job when I returned from Nigeria.

---

[27] "For God so loved the world that he gave his one and only Son, that whoever believes in him shall not perish but have eternal life."

[28] Isaiah 41:10a

It was such a shock. I was furious and felt betrayed by the management, but remained composed. My reply was, "Okay," in a calm tone, which surprised the manager.

She went on with what appeared to her as a normal conversation and said, "Are you not worried that when you return, you would wake up in the morning and discover that you have no job to go to?"

I replied, "What do you expect me to do? I came to find out why my annual leave had not been approved and you are telling me that my employment will be terminated on my return." I knew I had applied for my retirement with effect from the first week of April 2011, at the end of the financial year when all caseload midwives were expected to have completed their cases for that fiscal year. I did *not* know that I had been earmarked for dismissal or early illegal termination without proper cause.

My manager added, "You can appeal if you want to," to which I simply retorted, "I do not fight with management but God fights my fights," and walked out of the office. As I did so, I sent an arrow prayer to my army officer – Jesus.

"Dear Lord Jesus, I am confronted with a problem. You were aware of it before I was. I am handing it over to you right now. May your will be done. Amen."

This confrontation was unnerving because it was not something I had expected when I walked into the manager's office. Any human being would have felt the same, but confidence in the Lord was my bedrock – the knowledge that God is faithful, just and moves in mysterious ways. My inspiration was God's assurance that He would fight all my fights for me.

When you are afraid, standing on a shaky ground, remember that the God who created the shaky ground that frightens you also created you in His own image. He loves you so dearly that He will not allow the shaky ground to cave in beneath you for He calls you His beloved.

I informed my team leader and notified my clients. Some of them were very emotional and others requested a replacement midwife – something I knew was impossible because all the one-to-one (caseload) midwives had a full caseload for the year ahead. I had given notice and completed the documents for my retirement at the end of April 2011 at the completion of my cases. Why the management had decided to do what they did, I had no idea.

My colleagues and some members of staff gave me all sorts of advice to fight back but I put a brave face on it and did not show any signs of anger and concern. I knew what to do legally because I was a full member of the Royal College of Midwives (RCM) and the National Midwifery Council (NMC), which is our licensing body. I was familiar with all the relevant professional codes of conduct and accountability, had a clean disciplinary record, had never been the subject of complaints from clients and knew that the human resources accounts and salaries departments were all unaware of my manager's decision. Yet, though the law would clearly regard what had happened as illegal dismissal or wrongful termination of employment, that was not my intended line of action.

The following week, my first line manager returned from maternity leave and heard the story. She attended our weekly team meeting, and there I officially informed my colleagues about the termination of my employment. At that point my boldness gave way to the reality as my friends and colleagues were unable to control their emotions. Then my manager handed over the proper end-of-appointment documents for me to sign. The moment I received those letters, I was strengthened to move on.

The next thing left for me to do was to hand over my equipment and I planned to do so on my last working day that week. On the morning that I was going to hand over my equipment, I received a telephone call from my manager requesting that I should see her in her office urgently. I was not in any rush to see her earlier than the time I had planned to be in the hospital to hand over to her. Then another telephone call came, but still I did not budge because I wanted to show that nobody could intimidate me. I recognised that Jesus has all power and control.

When I eventually met my manager in the office at the time of my choosing, she said to me, "Do you want the good or the bad news?"

Polite and composed, I told her I could not care less.

Then she said that the senior management, including the director of midwives and the CEO had had a meeting in which they had heard about my case and decided that I should be reinstated. They wanted to go back on their previous decision as if nothing had happened. My long-standing annual leave application was approved and I was told I could carry on working after my retirement if that was my choice.

I told my manager outright that I accepted their decision of reinstatement but turned down the offer of continuing to work after my scheduled retirement.

She was persistent and wanted me back as member of her staff.

I said nothing, though my body language proclaimed, "I told you I have a supernatural power behind me in every circumstance, especially when I have done no wrong."

After thinking it over some more, I told her my clients were my priority and for that reason I would complete my caseload, since I did not want them to be let down and abandoned like sheep without a shepherd. Nevertheless, I remained adamant that I would not return to work after my planned retirement date.

To my surprise, my manager gave me two cards to wish me well, signed by the midwifery director and the midwifery managers, with two big, beautiful bouquets. Before I received their presents, I decided to make Jesus known to all of those who were involved in my case so that they would know that I worship a living God who is always in control in the lives of those who believe in Him. So I knelt down in front of her, raised my hands up to thank and praise the Lord Almighty in adoration, and said, "I am proud of the God I worship." She looked at me speechless. I received the cards and the flowers with gratitude because two wrongs do not make a right.

The manager who had given me the message of the illegal termination became the scapegoat and felt very uncomfortable whenever she saw me. One day, she met me in our break room and told me that what had happened was not her idea, but that others had put her up to it. I gave her a hug to show her how far the love of Jesus can go in forgiveness, as the Lord's Prayer teaches us.

Jesus broke all the chains that entrapped and entangled me so I will never be afraid of a fellow human being.[29] God said those who hope in Him will not be disappointed.[30] Though I did not start well in the beginning, yet He continues to work these miracles in my life through His beloved Son; such is His amazing grace!

I booked my flight to go home on holiday for three months from 31 May to 31 August 2011. As always, after the joy and happiness of reunion with family members and friends, the next question to expect

---

[29] See Acts 12:7
[30] See Isaiah 49:23

is, "When do you return to London?" Most of the time, there is no specific reason for that question, though I always feel obliged to give all the details of my movements. Unfortunately, I told everyone I was to return on 1 September 2011; it was a mistake that could have cost me dearly in time and money.

Throughout the three months I stayed in Nigeria, I was convinced that Saturday, 1 September was my return date, so I made last-minute appointments to make full use of my time on Friday, 31 August. That Friday morning, I had my normal quiet time to start the day before going out to finish off the things I had to do that day. When I was about to leave the bedroom after my prayers, I heard a voice say, "Why do you always think you are going back tomorrow?"

I mumbled, "Of course, I am going back tomorrow, Saturday."

The voice insisted, "Go and check your ticket."

Again, I muttered, "Why do I need to check my ticket?" Yet being aware of such mysterious encounters by now, I got my ticket from my suitcase. When I opened it, the first thing I saw was that my return flight to Heathrow was scheduled for Friday 31 August. Thankfully, it was not due to leave until 9 pm local time, so I had enough time to telephone around to cancel all my appointments. How can I quantify such goodness and love on the part of my Saviour? My High Priest knows all about me. Nothing escapes His wisdom and His knowledge of the sheep in His fold.

The Lord has continued to protect me day to day. In November 2015, I was deceived into financial loss by some unscrupulous people, but God the great "I AM"[31] intervened and saved me from the Internet rogues. Sometimes an existing problem can become an even bigger one, and that was my story in this instance.

My generation did not grow up with computers, though with the little knowledge and understanding we have, we try our hardest to get to grips with the basics. I received a phone call and the person introduced himself as a member of staff from Microsoft, offering free help and advice to people experiencing problems with their computers. He got my undivided attention because I was having problems with my laptop at that time. "What good timing!" I thought. He guided me step by step into giving him access to my laptop and gave me a fake website to operate it from my end. I noticed a lot of highlights that he claimed

---

[31] See Exodus 3:14b

were the faults in my laptop and he said that he was going to delete all of them. He then transferred me to another person whom he claimed to be the expert. This went on for some time and a third person came on the phone. He was the one to negotiate for the cost of the transaction, at which point I protested that it was supposed to be free. He replied that the charge of £11 was for my insurance, which had expired. I wanted to pay by debit card, but he insisted on being given my online banking number, which I had never previously used.

When I said no, I could perceive the frustration in his tone. As he realised that I was not going to give in to his request, he accepted the payment by debit card and the computer screen went blank at that point. He was still talking to me, but refused to explain why the screen was blank; suddenly it flashed back and I saw "£150".

I asked him why I saw £150 on the screen and he claimed it was for someone else. At that point I became a bit suspicious but the bad deed was done; I was deep in their trap because I had given my card details and also turned my mobile telephone off at their instruction as it is connected to my broadband. It was absolutely my fault – and a nightmare.

Eventually these criminals extorted more than £150 from my bank account. The bank confirmed that there was no response when they tried to contact me to authorise the payment by text message because my mobile telephone was switched off.

When the fraudsters turned my computer screen back on, I could no longer concentrate, terrified at what they might have done to me. In that confused state, I perceived a tall, heavily-built, grey-bearded old man, who shouted at me from behind my back, "Close the computer and run to the bank." It seemed as if that shout revived me from a stupor. I rushed to the bank and explained what had happened. When my account was checked, it was found that more than the £150 that I saw on the screen had been taken and transferred through Western Union to someone in India. The bank's fraud department promised to investigate and a fortnight later the bank refunded the full amount I had lost.

Initially I was embarrassed to talk about this, but I am now open about it because there are novices like me that might fall prey to such hurtful mistakes. I was lucky to get my money back, as these days most banks blame the victim and will not make refunds. Therefore, my advice is for everyone to be vigilant and resist the fraudsters' pressure, to avoid becoming a victim.

Several chances were given me in adulthood to become a Christian, but I spurned them. Until my bereavement in 2009, I had no idea of the importance and value of Jesus' invitation to build my faith in Him. Looking back, I see this was the result of making wrong choices in life and I wonder why I failed to follow the right direction from the outset. Perhaps it was because I was doing well and was beguiled by the prospect of a bright future and high status in my chosen profession. In Nigeria, although a qualified nurse's salary may not be much in comparison to what other professions pay, the vocation, dedication and services rendered are highly valued in society and in the country as a whole.

As I became a Christian, I grew to understand what it means to have faith in Jesus Christ as my Lord and personal Saviour. I cannot imagine life without Jesus now as I experience His radiance all around me and compare the changes in my circumstances since He came into my life. I see that nothing is irrelevant to Him. He is involved in the small things in my life no less than in the large. I am transparent in His presence and He knows all about me, both the present and what is yet to come. Nothing can be hidden from Him. That might sound scary, but it is the evidence of the presence and power of the Holy Spirit – an inheritance of all believers from the Father through Jesus. I am not claiming to be perfect because I identify myself with the Holy Spirit; I still make mistakes. The difference is that now I am open to accepting my mistakes, making amends through confession, fasting and prayers, as Jesus taught us to do. My encounters with the Messiah and His interventions in my life give me deeper insight into my faith. No wonder the Samaritan woman dropped her water pot at the well, excited as she was to experience the mystery of her life and to become the first in the town to have an encounter with the long-expected Messiah. Joyfully, she ran straight away to tell the Good News and invite all to come and meet Jesus. She was surprised that He knew every detail about her,[32] but just as He knew all about her, so also He knows all about me and you and everyone else.

---

[32] See John 4:1-42

Chapter Nine

Healing

In 2015 problems with my eyes were still very much on my mind, but God had everything in hand. On Sunday, 2 August 2015, I was crossing the green to church (not Christ Church this time, but St Alban's Church on nearby Acton Green, which had become part of the same multi-site fellowship). As I did so, I perceived a tall, slim young man in a white robe approaching quickly from behind me.

When he came parallel to me on my right, he said, "Today, as you are going to church, drop all your problems there and go home in peace and joy."

I replied, "Yes, as I am going to church today, I will drop high blood pressure, glaucoma, wheezing and breathlessness, and go home in peace and joy."

He was walking beside me, listening whilst I repeated everything over and over again till we reached the church building.

Many members of the congregation were outside chatting and I lost sight of the man as I started talking to a friend. When the service was about to commence, everyone went inside to worship. It was a good turnout, the atmosphere was joyful and I felt the presence of the Holy Spirit. The worship was awesome; the worship team played familiar songs and tunes, and I was particularly happy as I worshipped my Lord with gladness and adoration. After the service came to a close, people went for tea and coffee but the music continued and I stayed behind to enjoy myself.

I had not been that happy for some time: indeed. Then I re-membered it was past the time I needed to put in my eye drops. As I bent my head backwards to put the first drop in, I heard a prompting,

"Go and do that in the chapel. Drop all the problems you brought to the church there and go home in peace and joy." I did just that, sitting on a chair in the chapel to put my eye drops in. Then, standing in front of the cross, I made a gesture as if I was dropping things on the floor. I repeated what the man had told me to say, then went home.

At home I decided to put more eye drops in before having lunch. Within five minutes of doing so, I tasted an awful bitterness at the back of my throat that I had never experienced before. I could not eat my lunch immediately but had to brush my teeth and rinse my mouth several times before I could do so. As I was eating I had a strange sense of relief and comfort, located in a hollow below my sternum. The ease across my chest was amazing and I felt light, no longer tight and heavy. I was alone in the flat but I screamed, "Oh, my God! Oh, my God! I am breathing normally! I am breathing normally!" as if I was talking to someone else in the flat. I felt as though a heavy weight had been scooped out from my rib cage. That night, for the first time in ages, I slept without experiencing the horrifying respiratory problems I had become accustomed to.

Before I went to bed I prayed for the appointment I had at the hospital the following day to review my case, asking for this to show normal pressure in both eyes. And this was exactly what the Lord did for me. It was the shortest consultation I ever had. My next review was set for four months' time, and all medication was discontinued except the preservative-free lubricants that I use when my eyes are dry and itchy. That afternoon I came back home very happy and was relieved.

That same Monday night as I was praying before going to bed I heard a commanding voice, "Go and sleep with one pillow." This was a shock because up until then I had used four pillows and a couple of cushions and was still unable to sleep. Recognising the familiar prompting, however, one pillow is all I have used from that day onwards, and I have had no further breathing problems.

At my next hospital review on 22 February 2016, I had visual field tests in both eyes with good results, intra-ocular pressures were normal and this time my next appointment was set for six months' time, a year after my divine healing. All my medication was discontinued and I have recovered to my normal self and well-being. My GP also received a progress report confirming how well I have responded to treatment, stating that no deterioration has taken place in my right eye (the worse of the two) despite so many years of unstable pressure and a series of operations, including an implant. The gracious and Almighty God is powerful and good. I have an unstoppable love and faith in Blessed Jesus and have experienced the power and presence of the Pentecost Holy Spirit in my life.

The focus in my relationship with Jesus is on unfailing trust, obedience and response to the promptings of the Holy Spirit. At the beginning of my journey I regarded the voice of the Holy Spirit as my own imagination and always did the opposite of what He told me to do, with disastrous outcomes. As time went on, I discovered that it is through this voice and prompting that the Holy Spirit leads and guides individuals. The moment I perceived this and responded with confidence, I experienced the difference in my daily life. I am not boasting about having unique faith – not at all! – but I believe the timeless Word of God as the ultimate truth about the Holy Trinity as evidenced in the encounters I have related here. God created me in His own image,[33] engraved me on the palms of His hands[34] and gave His own beloved Son Jesus as ransom to be crucified for my own sins.[35] Through His resurrection I received God's amazing grace,[36] so I need no further explanation to prove that God loves me. The reason in John 3:16 is enough evidence to authenticate God's love for mankind and the Good News of the Messiah.[37]

In the prime of my life I was joyful and relaxed, without financial worries or fear of going blind, but as I grew older this became the reality. I learnt from my own experiences that life will never go as easily or smoothly as we might expect, especially with events that are beyond human control. There will always be ups and downs, twists and turns, and this is the background to our walk of faith. Faith is not being a Sunday Christian or getting involved in all sorts of church organisations and activities, as I did in my youth. It is about relationship. From the point of view of my own personal experience, I see it as a persistent and sustained self-satisfying journey with a focus on Jesus as Lord of my life and personal Saviour. It is not an easy journey, but worth persevering in, as my narrative shows. This faith journey has a beginning, but no

---

[33] See Genesis 1:27
[34] See Isaiah 49:16
[35] See Romans 5:8
[36] See Romans 5:17b
[37] See John 1:29-34

ending, and only through it can we witness that God is God and He never changes; that Jesus died for our sins, was buried in a rock-cut borrowed tomb, but brought back to life on the third day to give all people new life and a second chance; and He is still alive today. This Good News is spreading across the globe as believers are inspired and empowered by the Holy Spirit to witness the Great Commission He gave to His believers.[38] That is, you and me!

I could say much about the pain I experienced from deaths, hurt, disappointments, stillbirth and failed marriage, but looking back now, I appreciate my time of joy and happiness that a single death overshadowed. I thank God that through my misfortunes, I have learnt a great and most vital lesson: dependence on God through Jesus Christ as the only practical means of survival. As I was going through the panic and pain of bereavement, Jesus came into my life to shine the beam of His radiance into my darkness. He was the One who placed me on the right footing through the Holy Spirit, who led the way in all my encounters. The benefits of surrendering my life to Jesus and trusting Him outweighed all else and took away the pain that made me weak, unstable and fragile. Individual circumstances may vary, but my experience confirms that "Jesus Christ is the same yesterday and today and forever."[39] Today I realize that having Him in my life is like having a best friend in my heart that I was unaware of, and I can neither say nor do anything without Him at any time.

Even though I did not make a formal commitment or dedicate my life to Jesus at an early age, I was very much aware of the fact that He has power and authority from God His Father to heal all kinds of diseases, and I was hungry for His healing – not through physical touch or prayers, but by the mere fact of walking on the soil He walked and being baptized in the same water of the Jordan River that touched His own skin. What great expectations I had, and they were fulfilled! Despite my limited understanding, I did have faith, and that faith took me forward in God's purposes for my life. Faith needs determination and concentration to achieve the desired goal. Faith is a perspective, not comparable and never insignificant. It is not assessed by the magnitude of need but by trusting in Jesus without doubt. Jesus said nothing will

---

[38] See Acts 1:8
[39] See Hebrews 13:8

be impossible for us,[40] if we have faith as small as a mustard seed. Therefore, a culmination of need, faith and fruition bring about hope and wholeness. All that is required is to rely on His word, trust Him implicitly and be patient for the manifestation of our prayers and supplications. My advice is to read the Bible accounts of Jesus' life with an open mind, because these are packed with useful and encouraging material that will enable anyone to find pure love and real life in Jesus. The Holy Bible proves and confirms who Jesus says He is: one with the Father.[41]

---

[40] See Matthew 17:20
[41] See John 10:30

CHAPTER TEN

Calling

Some might have seen my career as my livelihood, but to me it was a vocation, a way for me to serve God through mankind. With the benefit of hindsight, I can see that God was working in me from my earliest years. In 1987 I found a yellow rumpled piece of paper on the desk in my office as I walked in for night shift. Nobody else was in the office. I was curious to see what was on the paper and who had left it on my desk. When I opened it I found a prayer that had been cut out from a magazine. It read:

> *Dear Lord Jesus, I am a sinner.*
> *I believe you died for my sins,*
> *And washed me clean with your precious blood.*
> *I accept, confess and repent of all I have done wrong.*
> *Please forgive me and come into my heart and life.*
> *Thank you for saving me. Amen.*

For many years, I was not aware of the importance of this prayer. All the same, I read it over and over that night, and by daybreak, I had memorized it. I used it routinely from that time onwards whenever I prayed, even though I did not know its significance and the impact it would have on my life. I did not know that it was a prayer of dedication to accept Jesus as my Lord and personal Saviour. The first time I realised this was when I was invited to a church event entitled "The Book of Life". At the end of the show, people were invited to come to the front to dedicate their lives to Jesus. I went forward. The pastor recited very similar words to the prayer I had found on my desk many years before and we repeated it after him. I was happy as I reflected on the prayer on that rumpled piece of paper. I thanked my friend for inviting me to the event and for the opportunity to make my dedication to the Lord there. I still have the lingering question, "Who left that paper on my table?" Now that I know the importance of this prayer, I regard it as a blessing from the day I found it because I used it from the start, even if not as it was meant to be.

Jesus was my motivation, skill, passion and hope at every birth. I give Him all the credit for making me the outstanding midwife that I was. My practice was not influenced by litigation or the social status of any client. It brought me no fame and I sought none. When I helped women in childbirth, the new parents-to-be and their families were always very anxious and apprehensive. At such moments, I saw how vulnerable expectant parents can be, and how much trust they put in me as their midwife. I would transfer that trust and their vulnerability onto Jesus because I perceived Him around me all the time. I saw my professional competence and skills as God's adorable gift and grace, His assignment to be part of His mystery in the life of every newborn – His creation. Though I expected safety and normality of all the births at which I assisted, I could never predict the mysterious process and outcome of a labour – but Jesus can because nothing is impossible with God.[42]

When I retired, I prayed and wrote a personal prayer request, asking the Lord to use me again wherever He wanted me to serve Him and His people according to His purpose, plans and desire. The title of the prayer is, "Lord use me":

> *Father, my midwifery career might have been seen as your provision for my livelihood. I perceived it as serving you through mankind, a vocation I am proud to be identified with.*
>
> *It was my joy but your grace to serve you in that way, and I am still willing to do more for you. You have preserved my life and also given me good health to continue serving you.*
>
> *I do not know where else you need me. If you believe that I am still useful, please, Lord, may you use me again for your other plans, purposes and desires, for I belong to you. Amen.*

---

[42] See Luke 1:37

Coming from the background I do and having had such unusual experiences, I believed these gave me great opportunities to be of further use to God, and on 26 February 2014, the Lord prompted me to give up all to follow Him. He has had such a great impact on my life, yet still I was unsure and felt inadequate to accept such a commission. After all, I had nothing special that I could forgo for His sake. Might it be my mundane body of dust and ashes? When I reflected and prayed about it, I realised this was my second chance and a further opportunity to serve the Lord. No job is too hard, small or big. When the Master places you in any situation, He will give the strength to perform well. Our part is to serve with diligence and joy. I am ready if He finds me useful for His purpose and desire. He has given me real life full of joy, happiness, smiles and peace. He is the source of God's limitless resources and provisions and also the channel of peace and abundance.

"God moves in a mysterious way," wrote William Cooper (1731-1800). I believe this book is a positive demonstration of answered prayer, as the Lord called me out of one profession to a new kind of service that will resonate with His love, might, compassion, faithfulness and grace. Whatever we have been, are today or will be in the future, our daddy still loves and cares about us. He cannot and will not be ashamed of us. If He is not ashamed of us, why should we be ashamed of ourselves? The moment we are able to release the pain within our hearts to Jesus, we will have no more fears or embarrassment because He is the only One who sees what we are hiding in our secret place, the heart. Hope and joy will well up inside us, while gloom and turbulence give way to worthy transformation.

When we focus on who and what God is, all that He created in His own image should have an obligation without reservation to honour, praise, worship, adore and glorify Him through Jesus, our One and only Mediator. "Be still and know that I am God; I will be exalted among nations, I will be exalted in the earth"[43] were His demands. When we trust and have confidence in Him, our faith will glow like an unquenchable fire. He has power, authority and control over everything for all of our needs. Personally, though I always embraced the fact that the power of light is much greater than darkness and that light is the fulfilment of a loving relationship with the Son of the Living God, if I had been perceptive about how to build faith in Jesus in adulthood, I

---

[43] Psalm 46:10

would have accepted Him into my life so much earlier than I did. I was unaware of the empowerment of the Holy Spirit and how much God impacted my life through my personal circumstances. I would have told these stories and testimonies of my encounters with Jesus much sooner, too, as a mark of appreciation, because He was the medium in all of them. They mark my transformation from being a Sunday Christian to a seven-days-a-week matured Christian. Now my worship is heightened and my faith journey intensified as I enjoy God's grace and abundant peace in my life.

Hitherto, I could not boast of having a faith in Jesus, but as a result of trials and tribulations I was able to respond to Him through the power and presence of the Holy Spirit. I have built an incredible faith in the Lord. Nothing I might possess can be worth more than life with Jesus of Nazareth. I love and trust Him because He loved me first. He gave me His life; I did not give Him anything. My story is all about Him and He is my perfect joy. This is why I witness to His power, love, compassion, faithfulness, authority and control in my life: to glorify Almighty God and encourage others.

Since giving my life fully to Jesus, I have carried Him along with me in every sphere of my life, not in my pocket or handbag, but at every point of the cross, because that is the reminder of what He suffered on my behalf. God intended salvation for all He created in His own image through His Son Jesus Christ, but not everyone understands and embraces this amazing grace and the abundance that comes with being in relationship with Jesus through the power and inspiration of the Holy Spirit. Younger generations might not comprehend true faith and what is required of them to be truly called Christians until they grow up to know the right path, learning from their own individual experiences, just as I did by following "the way, the truth and the life".[44]

I trust this book has been a source of inspiration and encouragement to you. The take-home message is to be patience and persevere in prayer, focusing on none other than Jesus. Yahweh is a promise-making and promise-fulfilling God. With Jesus as the medium, the Holy Spirit empowers individuals as they progress on their faith journey. Come one, come all to worship the Lord with those on the great Commission,[45] witnessing to the truth of the Good News of the Christ

---

[44] John 14:6
[45] See Matthew 28:16-20

who sacrificed His own life willingly on our behalf. The grace of God, a new life through the resurrection and the promise of eternity belong to those who walk with King Jesus. Shalom. Amen.

CHAPTER ELEVEN

Reflections

This book is all about the love of the Almighty God and not about me. I have told this story to explain how the Trinity impacted my life when times were hard, and to share some details of my revived life in Christ. I was healed, comforted, strengthened and showered with abundant peace and love through relationship with Jesus, even though at the time I was trying to overcome the hurdles of pain, brokenness, bereavement and darkness in my own strength. I hope this will be an encouragement and inspiration to other people who may be going through similar or worse circumstances. God is a loving, compassionate, faithful and righteous heavenly Father. We all have ample opportunity to seek His presence through Jesus Christ, His only begotten Son as our Mediator, and to receive empowerment through the presence of the Holy Spirit, our inheritance.

At the start of this book I never claimed to have a particularly great faith, but through my experience and trusting in Jesus' intervention I have discovered an incredible trust in the Messiah. This is grounded on a solid foundation that no storm can blow down because even the sea and the winds are obedient to Him.[46] This same opportunity is freely available to all who call on Him, for He is mighty to save.

In my hour of need I did not have the encouragement I yearned for because I was trapped in my own darkness, and this lack of openness on my part prevented my seeking divine help. It was not until Jesus intervened in November 2009, when He saw my brokenness and came in His love to bring me hope, that I broke out of this cage. He did this

---

[46] See Matthew 8:23-27

because He loves me dearly. He died on the cross, taking the punishment for my sinfulness so that I could be forgiven, and free to be reconciled to the Father. Through His resurrection, I gained God's grace, which I did not deserve. He invited me to follow Him, and the moment I accepted that invitation by making Him my Lord and personal Saviour, my life changed forever. I was not offered faith in Jesus on a silver platter, since we all have to make personal sacrifices in the course of life, but I focused on Jesus in good times and in bad – knowing Him to be faithful to His word and that He would always be there for me. "Do not be afraid, just believe,"[47] He said to His disciples. The Lord knows those who put their trust in Him, which is why the woman who had been bleeding for twelve years was healed instantly.[48] He never disappoints those who put their trust in Him because He is compassionate, faithful and righteous.

This book contains true accounts of my encounters with Jesus. These did not come about because of my involvement in church activities, or my diligence in reading the Bible and praying, nor even because of the extent of my love for Him. I am still slow at forgiving those who hurt me, even though I have received extraordinary mercy and forgiveness from the Father through Christ. He is nurturing me in His love and patience as I continue focusing on Him during my faith journey, until He makes me the child of His delight. I have no goodness in me but claim the goodness I find in my Lord and Saviour. I cannot fight principalities and powers, yet with Him on my side I have the armour of victory to fight all ill in His power and might.

Jesus is the perfect healer. His invitation is for *all* mankind because we are created in His Father's image and for that reason He was made the sacrificial lamb for humanity. My slate – everybody's slate – was wiped totally clean on His body and washed immaculate with His precious blood on the cross as He said, "It is finished."[49] From His own experience of Jesus, the apostle Paul wrote, "Nothing in all creation, on earth or heaven, can separate us from the love of God that is found in Christ Jesus our Lord."[50] Wow!

---

[47] Mark 5:36
[48] See Mark 5:34
[49] John 19:30
[50] Romans 8:38-39

I perceive Jesus as the only source from which to receive God's limitless resources and provision, as well as the ever-flowing channel of God's peace and abundance. My advice is to try Him. There is no waiting list, barrier or gate fee. He is a refuge without doors and walls, only a roof, and, "If God is for us, who can be against us?"[51]

---

[51] Romans 8:31b

What Shall I Read Next?

Tracing the Golden Thread
Mary Weeks Millard
ISBN 978-1-907509-49-0

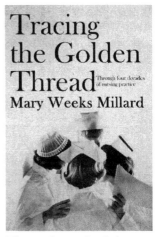

An inspiring story from the frontline of practical faith in action. Mary Weeks Millard, a quiet and unassuming girl, overcomes social shyness childhood illness and a poor educational start to aspire to her heart's call to become a nurse on the mission field. She tells her own unique and inspiring life story by painting a colourful and often graphic picture of training as a nurse and midwife in the UK in the 1950s. Pressing ahead against all the odds, Mary finds doors opening as she exercises her faith in a God of possibilities. These doors lead her to adventures and challenges of working in East and Central Africa in the years following independence and civil war before returning to equally challenging situations in UK.

Diamonds in the Darkness
Pat Nickson
ISBN 978-1-907509-14-8

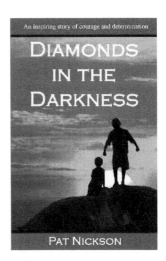

This book tells the story of a remarkable woman who made herself available to God wherever she went. After training as a nurse Revd. Dr. Pat Nickson OBE worked across the world from England to Australia, Bangladesh, Afghanistan and the Democratic Republic of Congo. Congo was her home for more than twenty-five years and the founding of IPASC (the Pan African Institute of Community Health) is her endearing achievement.

Books available from all good bookshops and from the publisher:
www.onwardsandupwards.org